THE SUMMITS OF GOD-LIFE:
SAMADHI AND SIDDHI

SRI CHINMOY

THE SUMMITS OF GOD-LIFE: SAMADHI AND SIDDHI

by
SRI CHINMOY

THE SUMMITS OF GOD-LIFE: SAMADHI AND SIDDHI

by
SRI CHINMOY

ISBN O-88497-145-7

Printed and published by:
AGNI PRESS
84-47 Parsons Boulevard
Jamaica, N.Y.

PREFACE

This book represents one of the very few genuine accounts of the inner universe — the universe beyond space and time, beyond all mental formulation. It is not a philosophical or theoretical book, but a vivid and detailed description of spiritual Reality by a Yogi who makes his home there. As a God-realised spiritual Master who has become one with the highest Truth, Sri Chinmoy is able to answer very specific questions on such subjects as liberation and illumination, samadhi, nirvana, bliss and the different planes of Consciousness.

By traditional accounts, one would expect to find an illumined Yogi in some Himalayan cave, lost in trance. But Sri Chinmoy is one of those rare spiritual Masters who seek to offer their Light not only inwardly, through meditation, but also outwardly, through the spoken and written word. This book consists of Sri Chinmoy's answers to questions asked by seekers at some of his public meditations and university lectures.

TABLE OF CONTENTS

ILLUMINATION

In this world there is only one thing worth having, and that is illumination. In order to have illumination, we must have sincerity and humility. Unfortunately, in this world sincerity is long dead and humility is yet to be born. Let us try to revive our sincerity and let us try, on the strength of our aspiration, to expedite the birth of our humility. Then only will we be able to realise God.

Illumination is not something very far away. It is very close; it is just inside us. At every moment we can consciously grow into illumination through our inner progress. Inner progress is made through constant sacrifice. Sacrifice of what? Sacrifice of wrong, evil thoughts and a wrong understanding of Truth. Sacrifice and renunciation go together. What are we going to renounce? The physical body, family, friends, relatives, our country, the world? No! We have to renounce our own ignorance, our own false ideas of God and Truth. Also, we have to sacrifice to God the result of each action. The divine vision no longer remains a far cry when we offer the result of our actions to the Inner Pilot.

In our day-to-day life, we very often speak of bondage and freedom. But realisation says that there is no such thing as bondage and freedom. What actually exists is consciousness—consciousness on various levels, consciousness enjoying itself in its various manifestations. In the field of manifestation, consciousness has different grades. Why do we pray? We pray because our prayer leads us from a lower degree of illumination to a higher degree. We pray because our prayer brings us closer to something pure, beautiful, inspiring and fulfilling. The highest illumination is God-realisation. This illumination must take place not only in the soul, but also in the heart, mind, vital and body. God-realisation is a conscious, complete and perfect union with God.

We want to love the world; the world wants to love us. We want to fulfil the world; the world wants to fulfil us. But there is no connecting link between us and the world. We feel that our existence and the world's existence are two totally different things. We think that the world is something separate from us. But in this we are making a deplorable mistake. What is the proper connecting link between us and the world? God. If we approach God first and see God in the world, then no matter how many millions of mistakes we make, the world will not only indulge our mistakes; it will soulfully love us as well. Similarly, when we see the defects, weaknesses and imperfections of the world, we will be able to forgive the world and then inspire, energise and illumine the world just because we feel God's existence there.

If we do not see God in all our activities, frustration will loom large in our day-to-day life. No matter how sincerely we try to please the world, no matter how sincerely the world tries to please us, frustration will be found between our understanding and the world's understanding. The source of frustration is ignorance. Ignorance is the mother of devastating frustration, damaging frustration and strangling frustration. If we go deeper into ignorance, we see it is all a play of inconscience. Frustration can be removed totally from our lives only when we enter into the Source of all existence. When we enter into the Source of our own existence and the world's existence, we are approaching the Reality. This Reality is our constant Delight, and Delight is the Breath of God.

This world is neither mine nor yours nor anyone's. Never! It belongs to God, and God alone. So we have to be really wise. We have to go to the Possessor first, and not to the possession. The possession is helpless; it can do nothing on its own. It is the Possessor that can do what He wants to do with His possession. So first we have to become one with God, and then we shall automatically become one with God's possessions. When we become one with God and with His possessions, we can certainly and unmistakably feel that the world is ours and we are the world's.

Ignorance and illumination are like night and day. We have to enter into illumination first, and then bring illumination into ignorance-night. If we try to illumine ignorance the other way around, then the transformation of ignorance will be difficult, slow and uncertain. To enter into the field of ignorance is to take a negative path. If we pursue the path of darkness and try to find light in darkness, we are taking the negative path. The best way, the positive way to find light is to follow the path of light, more light, abundant light, infinite Light. If we follow the path of light, then illumination will assuredly dawn in us.

Let us look up and bring down the Light from above. The moment we look up, God's Grace descends. The very nature of God's Grace is to descend upon each individual on earth. When we want to go up to God with ignorance, it is like climbing up a mountain with a heavy bundle on our shoulders. Naturally it is a difficult task. Instead of doing that, we can remain at the foot of the mountain and cry for God's Grace, which is ready and eager to come down to us from the highest. Needless to say, for God to come down into our ignorance is infinitely easier than for us to carry our ignorance up to God.

Illumination is the conscious awareness of the soul. Illumination is the conscious vision of the Reality that is going to be manifested. Illumination is possibility transformed into practicality. Illumination is like God's divine magic wand. An ordinary magician in this world uses his wand to make one thing turn into another. When God uses illumination in the world, immediately the finite consciousness of earth enters into the Infinite and becomes the Infinite.

Illumination is humanity's first realisation of God's omnipotent Power, boundless Compassion, infinite Light and perfect Perfection. It is our illumination that makes us feel what God really is. Before illumination, God is theoretical; after illumination, God becomes practical. So illumination is the divine magic power that makes us see the Reality which was once upon a time imagination. When illumination dawns in a human being, God is no longer just a promise, but an actual achievement.

Illumination is in the mind and in the heart. When the mind is illumined, we become God's Choice. When the heart is illumined, we become God's Voice. Here in the physical world the mind has evolved considerably. Because man has developed his intellectual mind, he has become superior to the animals, for the standard of the mind is higher than the standard of the physical or the vital. Man has cultivated the capacity of the mind, but he has not cultivated the capacity of the heart. When we cultivate the heart, we will see that its capacity is far greater than we had imagined. When we cultivate the unique sense in our heart that we are of God's highest Vision and we are for God's perfect Manifestation, then illumination will take place.

— Sri Chinmoy

CHAPTER 1

CONSCIOUSNESS, SIDDHI (GOD-REALISATION) AND INFINITY

Question: What is consciousness?

Sri Chinmoy: Consciousness is the inner spark or inner link in us, the golden link within us that connects our highest and most illumined part with our lowest and most unillumined part. Consciousness is the connecting link between Heaven and earth. Now, where is Heaven? It is not upstairs or somewhere far away. Heaven is in our consciousness. But it is the divine consciousness that connects earth with Heaven. The ordinary human consciousness will only connect us with something very, very limited and, at the same time, very fleeting. For one second we will be able to focus our consciousness on another person, and then our concentration disappears. But when we deal with the inner consciousness, which is the boundless, illumined, transformed consciousness, then our focus of concentration can go on, go on, go on.

It is not that only spiritual people have divine consciousness. Ordinary people have it also, but in them it is dormant. If they would concentrate, meditate and contemplate properly, this consciousness would come forward, and then they would have a free access to the soul, which is all Light, Peace and Bliss.

Consciousness is only one. It houses silence and it houses power. When it houses silence, at that time it houses its own true form. When it houses power, at that time it manifests its inner reality. A portion of the infinite consciousness that has entered into the gross physical and is possessed and used by the physical itself, we call the physical consciousness, the vital consciousness and the mental consciousness. In these there is a tiny portion of the infinite consciousness, but it is not the pure infinite consciousness that we speak of.

The eternal soul and the infinite consciousness must go together. They have a common friend, or you can say, a common father, and that is life, eternal life. One complements the other. The soul expresses its divinity through consciousness, and consciousness expresses its all-pervading power or silence through the soul.

Consciousness and the soul can never be separated, whereas the body can easily be separated from consciousness. What we, in our human life, call consciousness is usually only a feeling. When we perceive something subtle, immediately we call it consciousness, but it is not consciousness at all; it is a very subtle desire. We enter into the desire and immediately feel that this is our consciousness. Everything which is subtle in us and which we cannot define with words, we call consciousness; but consciousness is something totally different.

Awareness and consciousness are also two totally different things. If I talk with someone or mix with someone, then my mind becomes aware of his qualities. That is awareness. But consciousness is not a mental awareness or understanding. Consciousness is an inner revelation or an inner state of being. It is something infinitely deeper and more inward than awareness.

Question: What is the difference between human consciousness and divine consciousness?

Sri Chinmoy: Human consciousness is made up primarily of limitation, imperfection, bondage and ignorance. This consciousness wants to remain here on earth. It gets joy in the finite: in family, in society, in earthly affairs. Divine consciousness is made up of Peace, Bliss, divine Power and so forth. Its nature is to expand constantly. Human consciousness feels there is nothing more important than earthly pleasure. Divine consciousness feels there is nothing more important and significant than heavenly Joy and Bliss on earth. Human consciousness tries to convince us that we are nowhere near Truth or fulfilment. It tries to make us feel that God is somewhere else, millions of miles away from us. But divine consciousness makes us feel that God is right here, inside each life-breath, inside each heartbeat, inside everyone and everything around us.

Human consciousness makes us feel that we can exist without God. When it is in deep ignorance, human consciousness feels that there is no necessity for God. We see millions and billions of people who do not pray or meditate. They feel, "If God exists, well and good; if He does not exist, we don't lose anything." Although they may use the term 'God' in season and out of season, they do not care for the reality, the existence of God either in Heaven or in their day-to-day earthly lives.

But the divine consciousness is not at all like that. Even the limited divine consciousness that we have makes us feel that at every moment there is a supreme necessity for God. It makes us feel that we are on earth precisely because He exists. And when we cherish divine thoughts, the divine consciousness makes us feel it is He who is inspiring us to cherish these divine ideas. In everything the divine consciousness makes us feel that there is a divine purpose, divine aim, divine ideal, divine goal. In ordinary human consciousness there is no purpose, no positive goal; it is only a mad elephant running amuck. In the divine consciousness there is always a goal, and this goal is always transcending itself. Today we regard one thing as our goal, but when we reach the threshold of our goal, immediately we are inspired to go beyond that goal. That goal becomes a stepping-stone to a higher goal. This happens because God is constantly transcending Himself. God is limitless and infinite, but even His own Infinity He is transcending. Since God is always making progress, we also are making progress when we are in the divine consciousness. In the divine consciousness, everything is constantly expanding and growing into higher and more fulfilling Light.

Question: Could you please speak briefly about the different states of consciousness.

Sri Chinmoy: There are three main states of consciousness: *jagriti, swapna* and *sushupti. Jagriti* is the waking state, *swapna* is the dream state and *sushupti* is the state of deep sleep. When we are in the waking state, our consciousness is focused outward; when we are in the dream state, our consciousness is turned inward; when we are in the state of deep sleep, our consciousness is roaming in the Beyond.

When we are in the waking state, the identification that we make with anything or anyone is *vaishwanara,* that which is common to all men. When we are in the dream state, we identify with *tejasa,* which is our inner brilliant capacity, our inner vigour. And when we enter into deep sleep, there we identify with and experience the subtle. In this third state it is not the mental consciousness, not the intellectual consciousness, but the inner, intuitive consciousness that we deal with. In *sushupti* there is no collective form; everything is indefinite. It is all infinite mass. In this state we get an experience of a very high order.

There is also a fourth state, *turiya,* which

means the transcendental consciousness. This consciousness is neither outward nor inward; at the same time, it is both outward and inward. It *is* and it *is not*. It has the capacity to identify itself with anything and everything in the world and, again, it has the capacity to transcend anything and everything on earth. Furthermore, it constantly transcends itself. *Turiya* is the highest state of consciousness, but there is no end, no fixed limit, to the *turiya* consciousness. It is constantly transcending, transcending its own beyond.

The *turiya* state is like being at the top of a tree. When we are at the foot of a tree, with great difficulty we see a little bit of what is around us; but when we are at the top of the tree, we see everything around and below. So when we enter into the *turiya* state, we have to feel that we have entered into the highest plane of consciousness. From there we can observe everything.

In order to enter into the *turiya* state, for at least five or ten minutes every day we have to consciously separate our body from our soul. We have to say and feel, "I am not the body; I am the soul." When we say, "I am the soul," immediately the qualities of the soul come to the fore. When we are one with the soul, that state is a kind of samadhi. We can function in that particular state safely and effectively.

Nirvikalpa samadhi is also a state of the soul. When we have become one with the soul and are enjoying the eternal Peace, Bliss and Light of the soul, this is called *nirvikalpa* samadhi. In this state there is no thought. The cosmic play has ended; there is absolute Peace and Bliss.

In *sahaja* samadhi, while we are meditating, thoughts may be taking form in us, but we are not disturbed by them. In ordinary life we are disturbed by thoughts, but when we are in *sahaja* samadhi with the waking consciousness, although the earth sends a variety of thoughts from various angles, we are not disturbed by them.

Question: Would you please explain the seven higher worlds?

Sri Chinmoy: Deep inside us there are seven lower worlds and seven higher worlds. We are trying to transform the lower worlds into luminous worlds, worlds of perfection; and, at the same time, we are trying to bring the higher worlds into outer manifestation. Some of the higher worlds we already see operating in our physical world, on earth. First comes the physical, then the vital, then the mind, then the plane of intuition or the intuitive mind, then the overmind and the supermind. After the supermind comes Existence-Consciousness-Bliss — *Sat-Chit-Ananda.*

If you know how to observe them, you can see that some of these worlds are already functioning in you. During meditation, you can clearly see that it is not the physical world that you are entering into. It is something else: the higher mind or the overmind, or intuition or some other subtle world. But only spiritual Masters and great aspirants are conscious of the fact that these worlds are manifesting in their day-to-day activities, in the outer world itself. The ordinary person, even when flashes of intuition enter into his mind, will not be able to know that they are coming from the world of intuition. But each person, either today or tomorrow, has to become conscious of these worlds. Not only that, but also he has to manifest the truth, the light, the beauty, the wealth of all the higher worlds in this world.

You are a disciple of mine, and I can tell you that even now you sometimes get true, conscious, higher light from the intuitive mind. I know that your writings, your poems, come entirely from another world. From another world you are getting the truths and ideas which you express. I see that you get joy in writing entirely from the intuitive world, the higher mind. So, in the world of manifestation, the physical world, you are expressing the ideas, the light, the truth of another world. At the same time, if you want to enter into that world without manifesting, just to realise or see the vision of the truth of that particular world, you can. But for manifestation you have to bring this vision down here to earth.

Question: How can we tell which plane of consciousness we are in?

Sri Chinmoy: If you can meditate deeply, each plane of consciousness will present itself before you. Just in a flash it will come and present itself to you. The seven main planes of consciousness are like seven rungs of a ladder. As we aspire sincerely and soulfully, we climb up the ladder rung by rung. Or you can say that there is a tree with seven branches, and our consciousness is like a bird that flies from one branch to another.

When you are seated on one branch, you can see the next branch which is a little higher. Then, when you climb up to that one, you will see another one, which is still higher. Similarly, when you are making progress in the inner world, you will see these different planes, each one higher than the other. But when you are at the top of the tree, you are at a place where there is no limit, no distance above you. At that time, you are looking at the sky and you forget that the tree even has branches.

Right now if you try to learn about the seven planes of consciousness, your knowledge will be all mental and theoretical, a matter of curiosity. You feel that by knowing the seven planes of consciousness, or by concentrating on them, you will make rapid progress. But I wish to say that at this stage in your development it is not advisable for you to think of them or meditate on them. Always do the first thing first. Right now only pay attention to your own aspiration. For a sincere seeker, what is of paramount importance is conscious and constant aspiration. This conscious and constant aspiration can alone lead you to the destined Goal. Try to ask yourself this most significant question: "Am I ready to cry for God, the

Supreme?" As a child cries to the mother for food, so also you have to cry to the Supreme for Nectar. And if you can drink Nectar from Him, then you will be energised and your consciousness will be immortalised.

Question: When you meditate, some-times your eyes shift back and forth sideways very rapidly. Why do they do that?

Sri Chinmoy: This movement you see in-dicates that my soul is moving from one re-gion to another. Like a bird moving from one branch of a tree to the next, my con-sciousness is moving from one level to another. Each branch gives a special satis-faction to the bird: Light, Peace, Bliss, Power and so on. Similarly, each plane of consciousness I enter offers me its wealth, which I then bring down to my disciples and those meditating with me.

Question: What does God-realisation really mean?

Sri Chinmoy: God-realisation, or *siddhi*, means Self-discovery in the highest sense of the term. One consciously realises his one-ness with God. As long as the seeker remains in ignorance, he will feel that God is some-body else who has infinite Power, while he, the seeker, is the feeblest person on earth. But the moment he realises God, he comes to know that he and God are absolutely one in both the inner and the outer life. God-realisation means one's identification with one's absolute highest Self. When one can identify with one's highest Self and remain in that consciousness forever, when one can reveal and manifest it at one's own command, that is God-realisation.

Now, you have studied books on God, and people have told you that God is in every-body. But you have not realised God in your conscious life. For you this is all mental speculation. But when one is God-realised, one consciously knows what God is, what He looks like, what He wills. When one achieves Self-realisation, one remains in God's Con-sciousness and speaks to God face to face. He sees God both in the finite and in the in-finite; he sees God as both personal and im-personal. And in his case, this is not mental hallucination or imagination; it is direct reality. This reality is more authentic than my seeing you right here in front of me.

When one speaks to a human being, there is always a veil of ignorance: darkness, imperfection, misunderstanding. But between God and the inner being of one who has realised Him, there can be no ignorance, no veil. So at that time one can speak to God more clearly, more convincingly, more openly than to a human being.

As ordinary human beings, we feel that infinite Peace, infinite Light, infinite Bliss and infinite divine Power are all sheer imagination. We are victims to doubt, fear and negative forces which we feel are quite normal and natural. We cannot love anything purely, not even ourselves. We are in the finite, quarrelling and fighting, and there is no such thing as Peace or Light or Bliss in us. But those who practise meditation go deep within and see that there *is* real Peace, Light and Bliss. They get boundless inner strength and see that doubt and fear *can* be challenged and conquered. When we achieve God-realisation, our inner existence is flooded with Peace, Poise, Equanimity and Light.

Question: When you speak of seeing God face to face, what is your conception of God? Is He some being?

Sri Chinmoy: God is with form; He is without form. He is with attributes; He is without attributes. If an individual wants to see God as an infinite expanse of Light and Delight, God will come to that person as an infinite expanse of Light and Delight. But if he wants to see God as a most brilliant, most luminous being, then God will come to him like that. Of course, when I say God takes the form of a luminous being, I am understating the case. He is not merely luminous; He is something I cannot describe to you in human terms.

In my case, I have seen God in both ways — with form and without form. But when I speak of God, I speak of Him as a being, because this idea is easier for the human mind to grasp. When you say there is a form, a shape, it appeals to individuals. Otherwise, God becomes only a vague idea. If I say God is Bliss, and if the seeker has not experienced Bliss, then he will be hopelessly confused. But if I tell a seeker that God is like a person, an all-powerful father who can say this or do this, he can conceive of it and believe it.

When a human being thinks of some being greater than himself, immediately he thinks of it as similar to a human being. It is much easier to conceive of the idea of God through form. But I will never say that those who want to see God without form, as an infinite expanse of Light, Delight, Energy or Consciousness, are wrong. I just feel that the other way is easier.

Question: What part of man achieves realisation?

Sri Chinmoy: When realisation takes place, it is the entire being that realises God. The soul has already realised God, but the soul is bringing to the fore its realised consciousness. It is entering into the heart and trying to permeate the heart with its divine consciousness. Then, from the heart realisation comes to the mind, from the mind to the vital and from the vital to the physical body. When it envelops the physical, the vital, the mental and the psychic, realisation is complete.

Real realisation makes one know that one is neither the body nor the mind nor anything else but the soul, which is a manifestation of the Divine. Each person, when he realises God, will feel that he is a conscious portion of God. The physical is limited, but the soul is unlimited. When we speak of realisation, we are referring to something unlimited, infinite. When we realise God, we go beyond the body-consciousness and become one with the soul's unlimited capacity.

Question: I have read that realisation is not an achievement but a discovery.

Sri Chinmoy: It is not an achievement, but a discovery. But when we discover something, it then becomes our achievement. The moment we discover something, it becomes part and parcel of our existence; and whatever becomes part and parcel of our existence becomes our achievement. Right inside discovery, achievement looms large. When a scientist discovers something, it becomes the property of the entire world, but it is still his achievement. Similarly, when one realises God, although God has always been there and belongs to both the inner world and the outer world, God-realisation is still the most significant achievement for any individual.

Truth and Divinity already exist inside us, but we neglect them. Because we do not use

17

them, they have become foreigners to us. But the moment we discover them already within us, they become our own achievement. They become our achievement through our sincere personal effort and through God's constant inner Grace.

Question: Is realisation a fairly common experience during any single generation of human beings? In India, for example, are there many realised spiritual Masters?

Sri Chinmoy: There are millions and billions of people on earth, but only a very few of these are actually realised. If you feel there are hundreds of spiritually realised people on earth, then you are mistaken. The world is quite vast, but when it is a matter of truly realised persons, then I wish to say that there are only ten or twelve on earth right now. There are some swamis and teachers who have meditated and sincerely practised Yoga for ten or fifteen years, and who are far superior to their students, but who are not actually God-realised souls. One need not have reached the Highest to teach a beginner, just as one does not need a master's degree to teach kindergarten. To be very frank with you, these so-called Masters have indulged in doubt, impurity and other undivine things. But those who have really realised the highest Truth are infinitely above such self-indulgences.

There are sincere and insincere Masters. Many insincere Masters come to the West and exploit people. In India, also, false Masters exploit seekers. But God will not allow a sincere student to be deceived forever. The seeker's own inner cry will take him to a real teacher. If it is God's Will, the student may get a really high Master who will take him right from the beginning to the Highest. Otherwise, he will get a Master who will take him only through kindergarten, and then he will have to find another teacher.

Question: There are some paths which speak of the goal as enlightenment, and there are other paths which speak of the goal as God-realisation. What is the difference between enlightenment and God-realisation?

Sri Chinmoy: Full enlightenment, complete and all-illumining enlightenment, is God-realisation. But sometimes, when a seeker is in his highest meditation, he gets a

19

kind of inner illumination or enlightenment, and for half an hour or an hour his whole being, his whole existence, is illumined. But then, after an hour or two, he becomes his same old self; he again becomes a victim to desire and undivine qualities. Enlightenment has taken place, but it is not the Transcendental Enlightenment which occurred in the case of the Buddha and other spiritual Masters. That kind of all-fulfilling, all-illumining enlightenment is equivalent to God-realisation. God-realisation means constant and eternal enlightenment, Transcendental Enlightenment. When we get God-realisation, automatically infinite illumination takes place in our outer as well as our inner existence.

The enlightenment that is spoken of here in the West and also in Japan is only a temporary burst of light in the aspiring consciousness. After a short while it pales into insignificance, because there is no abiding reality in it. Abiding reality we will get only with constant, eternal and Transcendental Illumination, which is God-realisation.

Sometimes when we speak of enlightenment, we mean that we have been in darkness about a particular subject for many years and now we have inner wisdom, or

now that particular place in our consciousness is enlightened. But this is just a spark of
the boundless illumination, and that little
spark we cannot call God-realisation.

*Question: What is the relationship be-
tween realisation and the law of* karma?

Sri Chinmoy: When one realises God, one
has the capacity to stand above one's own
fate or *karma.* But if God wants him to
accept his own *karma* and go through the
pain and suffering, he will do so and offer it
as an experience to God. At that time, he
feels that God is having these experiences in
and through him. After realisation one can
nullify the law of *karma.* Again, if one wants
to accept the punishment or retribution of
others' *karma,* one can do it. If it is God's
Will, a realised person can nullify his own
and others' *karma,* or he can consciously,
deliberately and smilingly accept both his
own *karma* and the *karma* of others.

*Question: What is the difference between
seeing God and realising God?*

Sri Chinmoy: There is a great difference between seeing God and realising God. When we see God, we can see him as an individual or as an object or as something else. But we do not consciously and continuously embody Him and feel that He is our very own. When we see God, it is like seeing a tree. We do not at that time consciously embody the tree-consciousness. And since we do not embody it, we cannot reveal or manifest it. But when we realise something, at that time it becomes part and parcel of our life. We may see a flower, but only when we realise the flower do we actually become one with the consciousness of the flower.

When we merely see something, we cannot claim it as our very own, and that particular thing also will not claim us. Seeing is on the physical plane, while realising is on the inner plane. Seeing does not last, whereas realising does remain with us. If we see something, the vision may last for a short while; but when we realise something, this realisation lasts forever.

Question: When a person reaches the state where he achieves union with God, does his emotion or feeling of aspiration be-

come so intense that it automatically expresses itself in terms of words?

Sri Chinmoy: There will be no words at that time. You cannot express union with God in words; you can only feel it.

Question: Even if they are words of praise and oneness with God?

Sri Chinmoy: Yes, there can be words of praise and union. Human seekers often do express their spiritual experiences in words of intense beauty. Many spiritual figures have told us what union with God is, and mentally we think we know. But God-realisation cannot be expressed in the human tongue. One who has realised God is infinitely superior to an ordinary human being, and there are no human words to express his consciousness.

Question: After a person realises God, does he still act like an ordinary human being?

Sri Chinmoy: When we use the term 'realisation,' people are very often confused.

They feel that a realised person is totally different from an ordinary person, that he behaves in a very unusual way. But I wish to say that a realised person need not and should not behave in an unusual way. What has he realised? The ultimate Truth in God. And who is God? God is someone or something absolutely normal.

When someone realises the Highest, it means he has inner Peace, Light and Bliss in infinite measure. It does not mean that his outer appearance or outer features will be any different, for Peace, Light and Bliss are inside his inner consciousness. If a Master achieves realisation, it does not mean that he will grow two big horns or a long tail, or become in some other way abnormal. No, he is normal. Even after a spiritual Master has realised the Highest, he still eats, sleeps, talks and breathes just as others do.

It is inside the human that the divine exists. We do not have to live in the Himalayan caves to prove our inner divinity; this divinity we can bring forward in our normal day-to-day life. Spirituality is absolutely normal, but unfortunately we have come to feel it is abnormal because we see so few spiritual people in this world of ignorance. But this feeling is a deplorable mistake. Real spirituality is the acceptance of life. First we have to accept life as it is, and then we have to try to divinise and transform the face of the world with our aspiration and with our realisation.

Unspiritual people frequently think that a realised person, if he is truly realised, has to perform miracles at every moment. But miracles and God-realisation need not necessarily go together. When you look at a spiritual Master, what you see is Peace, Light, Bliss and divine Power. Enter into him and you are bound to feel these things. But if you expect something else from a realised soul, if you come to a spiritual Master thinking that he will fulfil your teeming desires and make you a multimillionaire, then you are totally mistaken. If it is the Will of the Supreme, the Master can easily make someone a multimillionaire overnight. He can bring down material prosperity in abundant measure, but usually this is not the Will of the Supreme. The Will of the Supreme is for inner prosperity, not outer affluence.

Question: How can one recognise a God-realised spiritual Master?

Sri Chinmoy: When you are with a God-realised Master, consciously or unconsciously you are bound to feel some Peace, some Light, some Bliss, some Power, because it is his very nature to radiate these things. He is not showing off; it is spontaneous, as the very nature of a flower is to emit fragrance. Every day you come in contact with thousands of people, but you do not get this from any of them.

A Master's outer body may be very ugly, but in his eyes you will see all divine qualities. And if his eyes are closed, you may observe nothing outwardly, but deep inside yourself you will feel an inner joy that you have never felt before. You have felt joy before, true, but the inner thrill that you will get the moment you stand before a real spiritual Master for the first time can never be described. And if the Master is your own Master, then the joy will be infinitely greater.

You are bound to feel all kinds of divine qualities in the spiritual Master, provided you have aspiration. Otherwise, you may sit in front of the spiritual Master, talk to him, have all kinds of intimate friendship with him, but you will get nothing. It is your aspiration that permits you to receive all the divine qualities of the Master. If you have no aspiration, no matter what the Master has, he will not be able to give it to you.

Also, when you speak to a real Master, your own sincerity has to come forward. This does not mean that you will always express your sincerity. You may tell lies in spite of the fact that your sincerity is pushing you, compelling you to tell the truth. But when you are with a spiritual Master, you at least *want* to offer your sincerity, although insincerity may come and fight with you and sometimes prevent you.

When you are with a realised Master, you are bound to feel that the Master understands you; and not only that he understands you, but also that he has the capacity to comfort you and help you in your problems. Some people feel that there is nobody on earth to understand them. But, if they are lucky enough to find a person who understands them, they come to know that this person still cannot solve their problems because he does not have inner light, inner wisdom, inner power. A spiritual Master not only understands your problems, but also has the capacity in infinite measure to help you in your needs.

When you stand before a Master, you will

feel that he can never be separated from your inner or outer existence. You feel he is your highest part and you want to grow into him. You want to become a perfect part of his highest realisation, for the very divine qualities that you are aspiring for — Light, Joy, Peace, Power — a spiritual Master has in boundless measure.

Question: When we reach liberation, does the physical body change?

Sri Chinmoy: The physical, vital and mental enter into the psychic consciousness when we are liberated. We do not discard them, but the physical, vital and mental aspire along with the soul. The physical, before liberation, is obscure and impure. In order for liberation to take place, the physical has to be purified. The vital is usually aggressive; before liberation it must become dynamic. The mind is usually suspicious; before liberation it must become vast and loving. These divinised parts of man enter into the heart when liberation takes place, and remain there permanently. The appearance of the physical body will be basically the same, but it will have infinite puri-

ty and luminosity, which it did not have
before.

*Question: Is there any difference between
liberation and realisation, or are they absolutely identical?*

Sri Chinmoy: There is a great difference
between liberation and realisation. Liberation is much inferior to realisation. One can
reach liberation in one incarnation, and
realisation in some later incarnation. Or one
can become liberated and realised in the
same incarnation. But it is not possible to be
realised without first being liberated. Sometimes a great spiritual Master, if he is fortu-
nate, will bring down with him a few really
liberated souls to help him in his manifestation. Sri Ramakrishna, for example,
brought down Vivekananda and Brahm-
ananda. Some of these liberated souls who
enter the earth-scene with the great Masters
don't care for realisation. They come just to
help. Others, like Vivekananda and Brahm-
ananda, want realisation also.

A liberated soul is liberated from ignorance, from worldly, undivine qualities. A
liberated soul will inspire others with his

presence. He will inspire them to be pure, simple, kind-hearted and loving. Tremendous purity and serenity will flow from him, and others will want to touch him, speak to him, look at his face. You can say that he is much more than a saint. True, worldly obscurities, impurities and other things will not enter into the liberated soul, or he will be all the time cautious so as not to allow them to enter into him. But a realised soul is much higher. He is consciously part and parcel of God.

A liberated soul knows that there is a special room where he stays and has his shrine. He knows that there is also a kitchen, which is all dirty and full of impurities. Ordinary human beings have no special room, no shrine at all. They are all the time locked in the kitchen, and naturally they cannot come into the room where the living deity is. The liberated soul is able to live in the room with the shrine, but he is afraid that if he enters into the kitchen, the undivine things there may attack him, and he will again become their victim as he was before his liberation.

But realised souls are extremely powerful. They know what they are and where they have come from. On the strength of their universal and transcendental consciousness, they can enter into the ignorance of humanity, into the earth-consciousness as such, and illumine it with their torch-light. They do so only because of their infinite compassion, not because they still have some temptations or wrong forces in them. No! They enter into ignorance deliberately so that humanity can be radically transformed. But only realised souls of a high order accept this bold challenge.

A liberated soul is like a child, so beautiful and pure. But how long can you stay with a child? With his capacity you cannot go very far, or reach the Highest. But a realised soul is like a mature person, who can offer you tremendous aspiration, light and wisdom, the living reality. A liberated soul will inspire you to walk along the path, but a realised soul will not only inspire you, but also guide you and lead you to your destination.

A realised soul is not only the guide, not only the way, but the Goal itself. First he pretends he is not even the guide, but just someone to inspire the seeker. Then he comes and tells the seeker that he is the guide, but not the road. Gradually, however, he shows that he himself is also the road. And finally he makes the seeker feel his infinite compassion and shows him that he is not only the guide and the road, but the Goal as well, the seeker's own Goal.

The realised soul touches the foot of the realisation-tree, climbs up to the topmost branch and brings down the fruit to share with humanity waiting below. That is realisation. But even the one who only touches the realisation-tree and sits at the foot of the tree without climbing up or bringing anything down is far superior to the liberated soul.

But again, to reach liberation is no easy matter. It is very, very difficult to become freed from ignorance. Out of the millions and billions of human beings on earth, there may be ten or twenty or even a hundred liberated souls. But God alone knows how many realised souls exist. To realise the highest Absolute as one's very own and to constantly feel that this realisation is not something you have actually achieved, but something you eternally are—that is called realisation.

CHAPTER 2

THE GREAT PILGRIMAGE:
HUMAN TRANSFORMATION

Man and God are eternally one. Like God, man is infinite; like man, God is finite. There is no yawning gulf between man and God. Man is the God of tomorrow; God, the man of yesterday.

— *Sri Chinmoy*

Question: Can a human being know the Infinite?

Sri Chinmoy: Certainly. If you could enter into my consciousness, you would realise the Infinite.

Question: But you are not infinite.

Sri Chinmoy: You are seeing me now as a man, but if you enter into my consciousness, you will see the Infinite Consciousness. If you meditate with me, I can enter into you and see the Infinite Consciousness within *you,* but right now you do not have that power. You are not only a human being with hands and feet; you have come from God, and you have within you all the possibilities of realising God.

Man in his outer life or his outer achievements is very limited. But the same man, when he enters into the inmost recesses of his heart, feels that there is something constantly trying to expand itself there. This is consciousness. This consciousness links him with the Highest Absolute. So when we ask how a man can achieve Infinity in his finite life, we must know that it is not in his physical body — in his arms or in his feet or inside his eyes — that he will achieve Infinity. It is in his inner consciousness.

Question: Do you believe that a human being can realise God and become one with Him here on this material plane, which is so ignorant and dark?

Sri Chinmoy: On the one hand, the planet earth is obscure, ignorant, inconscient; it does not care for anything divine. On the other hand, it has the tremendous inner urge to expand and transcend. God is aspiring through the earth-consciousness. Earth is the only place for people who want to be rich, either on the physical plane or on the spiritual plane. The life of desire and the life of aspiration are both possible on earth. Other worlds are for static enjoyment. In other worlds the beings are satisfied with what they have already achieved, whereas here nobody is really satisfied with what he has achieved. Dissatisfaction does not mean that we are angry with somebody or angry with the world. No! Dissatisfaction means that we have constant aspiration to go beyond and beyond. If we have a little light, we want to have more light, abundant light, infinite Light.

According to our Indian tradition, there are thousands of cosmic gods, and there are as many presiding deities as there are human beings. These presiding deities and gods remain in higher worlds—the vital world, the intuitive world or some higher plane. Right now they have more power, more capacity than we have, and they are satisfied with what they have. They do not want to go one inch beyond. But still, their capacities are limited in comparison with the Light, Bliss and Power of the Supreme. When we are liberated and realised, when we are consciously one with the Supreme's Consciousness, we will have infinitely more capacity than the deities and cosmic gods.

When the creation started, the souls that wanted to make progress followed a different path. They wanted the ultimate Truth, the infinite Truth. Even the cosmic gods, if they want to achieve infinite Peace, Light and Bliss, must come down to earth in human form and then realise God on the strength of their absolute love, devotion and surrender. Only here, in the physical body, can we pray and meditate and realise the Highest. Only this planet is in evolution. Evolution means constant progress, constant achievement. When one wants to make progress, when one wants to go beyond, then this is the place to come. It is here alone that God must be realised, revealed and manifested.

Question: What about the teachings found in some Western religions that one can see God only after death, if one has been good and goes to Heaven?

Sri Chinmoy: Heaven and God are not high above us, somewhere far away; they are deep within us, inside our hearts. Heaven is not a distant country where there are trees and houses and other objects; it is a plane of consciousness within us. Seekers of the eternal Truth will realise their eternal Heaven within their aspiring hearts. At every moment we are creating Heaven or hell within us. When we cherish a divine thought, an expanding thought, a fulfilling thought, we create Heaven in us. When we cherish undivine, ugly, obscure, impure thoughts, we are just entering into our own inner hell.

Question: Do we have to remove all materialistic goals in order to realise God?

Sri Chinmoy: How we utilise the material life is what is of paramount importance. Matter, as such, has not done anything wrong to God; it is not anti-divine. It is we who use material things in a wrong way. We must enter into the material life with our soul's light. We can use a knife to stab someone or we can use it to cut a fruit to share with others. With fire we can cook and with fire we can also burn ourselves or set fire to someone's house.

We have to feel that matter and spirit go together. Matter has to be the conscious expression of spirit. If you say that matter is everything, that there is no spirit, no higher life, no inner reality, then I have to tell you that you are mistaken. There is an inner reality, there is an infinite Truth that wants to express itself in and through matter. Matter is asleep, and it has to be aroused.

The material life has to be guided and moulded by the spirit.

But first we have to understand what the material life is for. If by material life we mean lower vital enjoyment and the fulfilment of gross desires, then it is useless to try to accept the spiritual life simultaneously. But if the material life means the life of expansion—the expansion of the heart, the expansion of love—then matter and spirit can easily go together. In this material life we have to see Peace, Light and Bliss. What we see right now in the mind is jealousy, fear, doubt and all undivine things. But in this very mind we can and we must feel harmony, peace, love and other divine qualities. If we want these divine qualities from the material life, then the material life can go perfectly well with the spiritual life.

The true material life is not just eating, sleeping and drinking. The material life is a significant life. And it eventually has to become a life of dedication. Right now in the physical we are trying to possess people and things. But the material life will have meaning only when we stop trying to possess and start trying to dedicate. When we dedicate ourselves to the Supreme, to the unparalleled goal of realising God, only then will life reveal itself to us as the message of Truth, the message of Infinity, Eternity and Immortality.

Question: Is technology acting as a hindrance to God-realisation?

Sri Chinmoy: The answer is in the affirmative as well as in the negative. When modern technology is serving as an expression of the inner soul, when it feels that it has a connecting link with the inner life, the inner existence, at that time technology is a help to God-realisation. But very often we see that technology and the inner life do not go together. The outer world with its success is running towards a different goal. We have to be very careful about this, for no matter how much success we derive from technology, the infinite fulfilment cannot take place if the soul is not there. Again, the soul is lame if the outer life does not keep pace with it through technological and scientific progress.

Science and spirituality have to go together, either today or in the distant future. Now they are at daggers drawn. But for the absolute fulfilment of God's Vision and

Reality here on earth, science and spirituality must go together. From spirituality we can expect liberation and realisation. From technology and science we can expect material perfection — the material embodiment of the highest Truth. When realisation is inside material success, only then will the material world achieve permanence in eternal values. Again, if perfection is lacking in the inner world, then the material success has to inspire the inner realisation to come and take the lead.

Question: Is it possible to have complete knowledge and wisdom of God in one lifetime?

Sri Chinmoy: It is absolutely possible to have complete knowledge of God, provided the aspirant has the most sincere aspiration. Also, the aspirant must have the capacity to hold the knowledge and wisdom of God. Third, the aspirant must have a very high spiritual Master, a God-realised Yogi of the first rank. Fourth, it must be the Will of God that the seeker receive this complete inner wisdom and knowledge. If all these four conditions are fulfilled simultaneously, then it is absolutely possible.

But if one just enters into the spiritual life and wants to realise God without the help of a Master, it is impossible. For an ordinary human being, hundreds and thousands of incarnations are required. Even if one has a good Master, if the disciple is not one hundred per cent sincere, it may take six, seven, ten or twenty incarnations. But the very best disciples get realisation either in one incarnation or in a few incarnations, under the constant guidance of the Master.

Occasionally someone realises God without having a spiritual Master. How is it possible? In his past incarnation, perhaps he had a very, very powerful Master. In this incarnation his Master has not taken human incarnation, but from the inner world this Master is constantly guiding him, moulding him and instructing him. The seeker knows that his Guru is instructing him during his dreams and during his meditation.

Then, of course, there is also another possibility. If a seeker has been meditating for quite a few incarnations and God is most pleased with him, and if the seeker is not favoured with a spiritual Master in this incarnation, then God Himself plays the part of a spiritual Master, even during the seeker's waking hours and in his day-to-day life activities. If the seeker needs to drink a glass of water, God will tell him, "Go and drink a glass of water." And if he has to shut the windows, God will tell him. God will take the form of a very, very luminous being and will guide him in this way.

Question: If a seeker does not realise God in this lifetime, does this mean all his efforts will be lost?

Sri Chinmoy: If a seeker does not attain to spiritual perfection in this life, that does not mean that he will lose everything. When he does not complete his journey in this life, in his next incarnation he starts the journey where he left off. Nothing is lost. But unfortunately, for the twelve or thirteen years of his childhood, he will be captured by ignorance. Ignorance will stand right in front of him and devour him like a wolf. He will have to take strength from the inner world and then fight like a warrior in the battlefield of life to conquer ignorance once again. But one who has realised God and attained perfect perfection in his previous incarnation does not have to wait all these years. So it is better to conquer everything in this life, so that in our next incarnation we can travel forward from the very beginning.

Question: Is it proper to have a motivation for achieving realisation, such as the desire for liberation? Is this a proper motivation?

Sri Chinmoy: Certainly it is a proper motivation. There are two different approaches to God-realisation. One approach is to make a complete surrender to the Will of God. This surrender has to be dynamic. Otherwise, you will be like the millions of lethargic people on earth, wallowing in the pleasures of ignorance, who are waiting for realisation at God's Hour. It will take these people millions of years to realise God, for if they do not utilise the capacity God has given them, then why should God play His role? In dynamic surrender, we play our role and utilise the capacity God has given us; then we leave it up to God to give us what He wants when He wants. In dynamic surrender, we make a full personal effort and then pray for the divine Grace. An ordinary person wants to achieve his goal by any means, by hook or by crook. But in the spiritual life, we do not do this. We use our patience.

The other approach is to have some idea of what we want when we are praying and meditating. Let us say I want to be good. This is quite legitimate. If I become good, that means there will be one less rascal on earth, and God's creation will be better. So I am praying to God to give me something which will help Him in expanding His own Light on earth. In order to be of some service to mankind and to please God in God's own way, we have to become good. But only when we realise God, can we be of real help to Him. Unless we are realised, unless we are free from the meshes of ignorance, what can we give to humanity? Unless we have some Peace, Light and Bliss, how can we help either God or mankind? There are many false teachers on earth who are not of any real help to mankind. They are like mushrooms growing all over the world. Now what are they doing? They are only exploiting and deceiving humanity. They can deceive themselves, they can deceive humanity, but they cannot deceive God.

The great spiritual Master Sri Ramakrishna used to pray, "O Mother Divine, make me the greatest of the Yogis." Ordinary people will say, "What kind of Master prays to be the greatest?" But this was not competition on Sri Ramakrishna's part. He just knew that if he could become divinely great, then he could be of real service to mankind. So there is nothing wrong in praying for realisation and liberation. If you do not have any motive, if you do not feel any inner hunger for God or for Peace, Light and Bliss, then God will say, "Sleep, My child, sleep, as millions and billions of other people on earth are sleeping."

Question: Is there a specific way to accelerate realisation?

Sri Chinmoy: Yes, there is a specific way, and it is called conscious aspiration. God must come first. There must be no mother, no father, no sister, no brother — nothing else but God, only God. True, we want to see God in humanity, but first we have to see Him face to face. Most of us cry for money, name, fame, material success and prosperity; but we do not cry even for an iota of inner wisdom. If we cry sincerely, devotedly and soulfully for unconditional oneness with our Inner Pilot, then today's man of imperfection will be transformed into tomorrow's God, the perfect Perfection incarnate.

Aspiration, the inner cry, should come from the physical, the vital, the mind, the heart and the soul. Of course, the soul has been aspiring all the time, but the physical, vital, mental and psychic beings have to become consciously aware of this. When we consciously aspire in all parts of our being, we will be able to accelerate the achievement of liberation.

How do we aspire? Through proper concentration, proper meditation and proper contemplation. Aspiration covers both meditation and prayer. In the West, there were many saints who did not care for meditation; they realised God through prayer. He who is praying feels he has an inner cry to realise God, and he who is meditating also feels the need of bringing God's Consciousness right into his being. The difference between prayer and meditation is this: when I pray, I talk and God listens; and when I meditate, God talks and I listen. When I pray, God has to listen. But when I meditate, when I make my mind calm and quiet, I hear what God has always been saying to me. So both ways are correct.

Conscious aspiration is the first thing we need. Aspiration is all that we have and all that we are. Then consciously, we have to offer our aspiration to the Supreme so that we can become one with Him.

Question: How do you achieve perfection?

Sri Chinmoy: Each time you aspire, I wish to tell you that your perfection is increasing. Inside your aspiration, perfection is growing and glowing. Sincere aspiration means the opening of the perfection-lotus. A lotus, you know, has many petals. Each time you aspire most soulfully, one petal of the lotus blooms. And when one petal blossoms, it means perfection is increasing in the entire lotus.

Right now, your idea of perfection, your goal, is realisation. That is your height of perfection. But when you realise God, at that time your aim will be to manifest God through your nature's transformation. Realisation is transformation into perfection; but complete perfection is the transformation of the human nature into the Divine Nature. There have been quite a few Masters who never cared for the transformation of their nature. This is a more difficult task than realisation. But nature's

47

transformation is real perfection, for by bringing down divinity into your earthly human nature, you will be perfecting your outer life, which is a portion of the outer world.

Question: Could you speak on the role desire plays in the movement toward God-realisation?

Sri Chinmoy: We often feel in our daily experience that desire is one thing and God is something else. Desire, we say, is bad in the spiritual life, for when we desire something, we feel it is the object itself that we desire. It is true that through aspiration alone we can realise God, but we have to know that God abides in our desire as well as in our aspiration. When we come to realise that desire also has its existence in God, we get our first illumination.

Our earthly journey starts with desire, and in the ordinary life we cannot live without it. But if we feel that we are not ready for the spiritual life just because we have teeming desires, then I wish to say we will never be ready for the spiritual life. We have to start our spiritual journey here and now, even while we are walking along the path of desire.

Let us take desire as an object and try to feel the Breath of God inside it. Slowly and unmistakably the Breath of God will come to the fore and transform our desire into aspiration. Then, if we apply this process to aspiration as well, we will come to feel that our aspiration and our earthly existence can never be separated.

There are two kinds of men on earth who do not have desire: those who have liberated souls and those who have dull, inert, lifeless souls. Liberated souls have freed themselves from bondage, limitations and imperfections. They have become free from ignorance and have become one with their souls in transcendental illumination. Again, some human beings want nothing from life. They just wallow in the pleasures of idleness and lethargy; they have no aspiration for anything. So they will never, never have illumination.

The great spiritual hero, Swami Vivekananda, was once asked by a young man how he might realise God. Vivekananda said, "From now on start telling lies." The young man said, "You want me to tell lies? How then can I realise God? It is against spiritual principles." But Vivekananda said, "I know better than you. I know what your standard is. You won't budge an inch; you are useless, you are practically dead to the ordinary life, not to speak of the spiritual life. If you start telling lies, people will pinch you and strike you, and then you will exert your own personality. First you have to develop your own individuality and personality. Then a day will come when you will have to surrender your individuality and personality to the divine Wisdom, the infinite Light and Bliss. But you have to start your journey first."

There is another story about a man who came to Swami Vivekananda and asked him about God-realisation. Vivekananda said, "Go and play football. You will be able to realise God sooner if you play football than if you study the *Bhagavad-Gita*." Strength is required in order to realise God. This strength need not be the strength of a wrestler or boxer, but the amount of strength required for normal day-to-day life is absolutely necessary.

There are some unbalanced persons who feel that they will realise God by walking along the street like a vagabond or by torturing their body and remaining weak.

Their physical weakness they take as a harbinger of God-realisation. The great Lord Buddha tried the path of self-mortification, but he came to the conclusion that the middle path without extremes is the best. We have to be normal; we have to be sound in our day-to-day life. Aspiration is not one thing and our physical body something else. No! Our heart's aspiration and our physical body go together; the physical aspiration and the psychic aspiration can and must run together.

Question: I have recently become your disciple, and I was wondering if it would help my progress if I kept thinking about my Goal of God-realisation.

Sri Chinmoy: A kindergarten student's ultimate goal is to get a Master's degree. Now, while he is studying the kindergarten lessons, if he constantly thinks, "Oh, I have to get my Master's degree, I have to get my Master's degree," it is foolishness on his part. He may know his goal, but if he thinks about it all the time, then he will not learn his present lesson well. There are some aspirants who think of God-realisation although they are not ready even for basic inner awakening. There are some who think and speak of God-realisation, whereas they are not yet ready even to learn the ABC's of the spiritual life.

God-realisation, Immortality, Infinity, Eternity: these are all big words right now. If you speak about these words, you will only be building castles in the air. They are a reality in their own plane, but that reality you cannot bring into your day-to-day life right now. So let the reality remain in its proper place. If you go on thinking of the Goal all the time with your imagination, the Goal will not be the way you are imagining it, and you are bound to be disappointed. Also, if you think of the Goal all the time, then you will not pay proper attention to your present aspiration and you will unconsciously delay your progress. God-realisation is your Goal, but you have just entered into the spiritual path. You are walking along the right path, and this is good. Right now your main concern should be aspiration, inner progress, simplicity, sincerity, purity and humility.

God-realisation is a difficult goal, but it is not impossible. After meditating for several years, some people feel that God-realisation is impossible in this incarnation and say that they do not want it. It is like the story of sour grapes. Many people leave the spiritual path for this reason after following it for quite a few years. They find fault with God and with the Master's teachings, and become stark atheists. But this is very bad. Before you entered into the spiritual life, when you were wallowing in the pleasures of ignorance, at that time God forgave you because He knew that you were not aware of anything else. God said, "My child does not know anything better than ignorance." But after you have entered into the inner life, if you go back again to the ordinary life thinking that God-realisation either does not exist or is totally beyond your capacity, then the inner retribution for your ignorant and undivine actions is infinitely worse than it would have been if you had never left ignorance at all.

Right now the Goal is a far cry, but you must not be discouraged. Step by step, slowly and steadily, you will reach the Goal. From kindergarten you go to primary school, then to high school and then to the university. So do not be restless or impatient. Only God knows when the choice Hour will strike for you. It is your business to aspire, and it is God's business to pour down His infinite Compassion. When you play your role, God will play His role and make you realise Him at His choice Hour. So let us walk along the path of reality. On the strength of our inner aspiration, the Goal itself will come toward us.

Question: Once a seeker becomes advanced, do all the obstacles to God-realisation vanish and does his realisation become a certainty in this incarnation?

Sri Chinmoy: Until you reach the Goal, there is no certainty. You may even be only one step from the Goal, and still you may fall. Even at the last moment you do not know whether you are going to win the race or not. Before God-realisation, the last trial is extremely difficult. Many really sincere seekers are about to realise God — believe me, in the inner world there is no more than an inch gap — but hostile forces attack them mercilessly and they fall. Then it takes such a long time for them to get up again. Some people take six months or two years or four years; others may have to wait for another incarnation. So always be on the alert and run as fast as you can toward your Goal. Do not stop until the race is won; otherwise, the pull of ignorance will take you back again to the starting point.

Question: When I think of all the failings and undivine qualities in myself and my fellow disciples, illumination seems a million miles away.

Sri Chinmoy: When one is really illumined, one will not see others as imperfect or hopeless human beings. The moment one is illumined, he will feel his real oneness with others and he will see the so-called imperfections of others as an experience God is having in and through them.

Since you are my disciple, I wish to tell you that you see more imperfection, more limitation, more teeming night inside yourself than I can even imagine. To me you are absolutely natural and normal; you are God's child, and you have every opportunity and capacity to realise, manifest and fulfil the Divine here on earth. Illumination is something which you had, but which you now have forgotten; it is not something totally new.

One who really cares for illumination has to feel that he is growing from light to more light to abundant light. If a seeker always feels that he is deep in the sea of ignorance, then I wish to say that he will never, never come out of ignorance, for there is no end to the ignorance-sea. But if one feels that he is growing from an iota of light into the all-pervading, highest Light, then illumination immediately seems easier and more spontaneous.

Question: Can we actually feel our realisation coming, or does it appear spontaneously and unexpectedly?

Sri Chinmoy: Real realisation cannot dawn unexpectedly. Gradually, gradually we come to the point where we realise God. If one is on the verge of realisation, he will know that it is a matter of days or months or years. Realisation is complete conscious oneness with God. Now if one does not have a *limited* conscious oneness with God, how can he attain an *unlimited* conscious oneness with God all at once? It is true that God can do everything, that He can grant realisation without asking anything of the seeker.

But if God did that, He would be partial. If God gave you realisation without your meditating and practising the spiritual life, then everybody would expect it.

Some people get realisation after only four or five years of meditation, whereas others who have been meditating for thirty, forty or fifty years are nowhere near realisation. But you have to know that in the case of the person who realises God after having meditated for only four or five years, this is not his first incarnation as a seeker. He started his journey long, long before you may even have thought of God. Now he is completing his journey to God-realisation, while you perhaps have just started yours. Again, we have to know that even though we have meditated for many incarnations in the past and for a few years in this incarnation, it does not actually mean that we deserve God. It was God's Grace that operated in our previous incarnations and it is God's Grace that is helping us realise Him in this incarnation as well.

From your constant, lifelong meditation, you can expect realisation, but only at God's choice Hour. You may want it immediately, but God may know that if you realise Him right now, you will be more harmful than helpful to mankind. So God has His own Hour for your realisation, and when that Hour nears, you will be aware of it.

Question: How do you know that there is such a thing as realisation, and how do you know when you are realised?

Sri Chinmoy: Many people have realised God. This is not my theory; this is not my discovery. Indian sages, Indian spiritual Masters of the hoary past, have discovered the Truth; and I also see eye to eye with them on the strength of my own realisation.

When you eat a mango, you know that you have eaten it. You have eaten a mango and the knowledge of it remains inside you. If others say, "No, you have not eaten a mango," it does not bother you, for you know what you have done. As long as your hunger is satisfied, you do not need the approval or recognition of others. The delicious taste, the experience that you had, is proof enough for you. In the spiritual world also, when one has drunk the Nectar of realisation, one knows that one has really realised God. One feels infinite Peace, infinite Light, infinite Bliss, infinite Power in his inner consciousness. A realised person can see, feel and know what Divinity is in his own inner consciousness. When one has realisation, he has a free access to God and a sense of complete fulfilment. When realisation dawns in an aspirant's life, then he will know it unmistakably.

Question: After a disciple has realised God, will he always serve you in the inner world?

Sri Chinmoy: After you have realised God, why should you serve me? You will not serve me, but you will serve God, the Supreme, the boundless infinite Consciousness. If you serve the infinite Consciousness of the Supreme, you serve me, because I am part and parcel of that infinite Consciousness; that is where I dwell in my inner life. But whom will you actually be serving? You will not be serving me, you will not be serving the Supreme; you will be serving yourself, your own highest aspect. The Supreme is not a third person, and I am not a third person. Once we are realised, we are all one. On the strength of your highest oneness with the infinite Consciousness, you will be serving the

One in three forms: the Supreme in His own aspects, the Supreme as your spiritual teacher and the Supreme as yourself. But the personality, the individuality that I have in this incarnation, you will not serve when you have realised the Highest.

Right now I am serving, serving, serving. I am serving my disciples and trying to manifest the Supreme on earth. Right now you, my disciples, have a little faith in me; that is why you are trying to manifest the Supreme. But practically nobody is serving Him consciously. If you had really been serving the Supreme, by this time you could have offered abundant Light to the world at large. You are serving in a way, but not spontaneously, wholeheartedly and lovingly.

When you realise God, at that time you will really know me. Now you do not know me. Among my disciples, not even a single one knows me. You say, "Sometimes Guru goes into a very high consciousness," but you do not actually know where my consciousness is. What I am you will realise only the day you realise God, not one second before. Right now when I talk of Infinity or Eternity, it is all meaningless to you. Some of you, with great difficulty, try to digest what I say, but you find it difficult to assimilate. But when you realise God, at that time you will understand me.

Question: Most of the time during my meditation I find myself walking inside a spiral. Does this have any relationship with inner realisation?

Sri Chinmoy: This has nothing to do with realisation. It is only an experience you are getting on your way. The spiral movement does not indicate realisation; it comes as an experience, as a good experience. It is the cosmic movement that you are seeing. Through the cosmic movement eventually one can realise God. Experience is the pathfinder of realisation, but it is not the beginning of realisation; it is not a form of realisation. It is only an experience.

Question: Could you elaborate on the difference between experience and realisation in the spiritual life?

Sri Chinmoy: The difference between experience and realisation is this: a realised person can say, "I and my Father are one," or "God and I are one," whereas an aspirant who has had many spiritual experiences can only feel that he is slowly but inevitably growing into the realisation of God. Conscious union with the Highest is called realisation. But if we get just a glimpse of the highest Truth, this experience is infinitely inferior to realisation. Experience tells us what we will eventually become. Realisation makes us conscious of what we truly are: absolutely one with God, forever, through Eternity.

It is good to have an experience, but we have to know that experience does not last. It is better to have realisation, even if this realisation is not total realisation and does not completely change our nature. Realisation is infinitely better than experience. Experience is a fleeting joy; realisation is a lasting joy. But even this lasting joy does not necessarily have all the divine qualities, such as Peace, Power and Wisdom. When we embody the Vision in its totality, we go one step deeper. The embodiment of Truth gives us infinite confidence in our inner life as well as our outer life. Again, mere embodiment is not enough. We have to reveal the Vision. Someone may have power, but unless he brings this power to the fore and reveals it, it cannot fulfil him either here on earth or there in Heaven. Again, even though we reveal without what we have within, revelation is not the final stage. The final stage is manifestation. What we have and what we are must be manifested here on earth. When manifestation is accomplished, then all is done.

Question: Are all our experiences transitory?

Sri Chinmoy: In the outer world we don't remember in detail all of our experiences. They are real for a few days and then they are totally erased, because they do not stay in our day-to-day consciousness. But we keep the essence of these experiences in our inner life. In the inner world, everything is recorded permanently.

Question: What about an experience we had in the inner world, such as an experience during meditation? Do we remember this consciously?

Sri Chinmoy: In the case of an ordinary seeker, when he has some inner experience, he does not consciously retain it, even though the essence remains in his inner life. Even if it is a high experience, after four years or so he totally forgets it. The experience is lost because the ignorance in his life swallows it. He says, "How can I have had such an experience? If I did have such an experience, how is it that afterwards I did so many wrong things? How is it that I did not meditate, I did not pray? That means it was not such a significant experience." His doubt devours the experience. But in the case of a realised person, he knows that whatever he saw or felt was absolutely true. Also, he can remember the inner experiences that he had even at the age of seven or eight, or in previous incarnations, because of his inner vision. But ask an ordinary seeker, and even if he has had only two major experiences in his life, it may take him an hour to remember, or he may not remember them at all.

Question: So after one realises God, he remembers all his experiences?

Sri Chinmoy: When one realises God, it does not mean that he will remember all the millions and billions of outer experiences he has had during his lifetime. But his inner experiences, the significant higher experiences that he had in the inner world, he can bring to the fore at his command. If he wants to bring his whole inner life in front of himself, he can.

Question: Is the experience of the Beyond calm or excited?

Sri Chinmoy: The experience of the Beyond is calm, but it is not static. In it, dynamism and tranquility exist together. In one of the Upanishads we find this definition of the Beyond: "That moves and that moves not. That is far and that is near." How can something move yet move not? It seems impossible. But when you are in the Beyond, you will see the universe in movement and, at the same time, tranquil. There is also another description of the Beyond: the experience of the Infinite. "Infinity is that. Infinity is this. From Infinity, Infinity has come into existence. From Infinity, when Infinity is taken away, Infinity remains."

Question: Who is the Unmanifest?

Sri Chinmoy: You yourself are the unmanifest. That is to say, your highest Self is still unmanifest. You, who represent God on earth, and you, who in your highest consciousness are absolutely one with God, are still unmanifest. Your highest is not manifested right now, but this does not mean that it will always remain unmanifested. No, your highest has to be manifested on earth, for then only can the perfect Perfection of the Supreme take place.

Question: Can a seeker live in vast expansion of mind, or is this possible only for a realised soul?

Sri Chinmoy: Vast expansion of mind the aspirant can have for a few minutes when he is in a very high, deep meditation. Only the realised soul can enter into this vast expansion of mind and stay there indefinitely. But we are actually making a mistake when we use the term 'expansion of the mind.' In the state I am referring to, there is no mind; the mind has been transcended. We feel that what we experience is the expansion of the mind, but it is actually the transcendence of the mind. In the mind there is form, there is limit; but when we speak of the vast expanse, it is something beyond the domain of the mind. It is a vast expanse of Light, Consciousness, Peace, Bliss.

When we are meditating, we always try to go beyond the mind. When we want to expand our consciousness, our physical reality, we have to enter into the soul. But when we come back from the highest level of consciousness, we try to understand and express the state we were in with the help of the mind. That is because the mind right now is the highest product of human life. But because the mind is limited, it can never understand and express the Infinite, the unlimited.

Question: Are the kinds of experiences that Yogis have different from those ordinary people get in life?

Sri Chinmoy: Sri Aurobindo once said that the biography of a spiritual Master is all written inside. If you write the biography of an ordinary person, it can be thousands of pages long. But if you want to write about his inner life, you will not be able to fill even one page. But in the case of a spiritual Master, hundreds and hundreds of pages can be written about his inner life, but they are not written. A spiritual Master, who is dealing with the inner world, gives and receives hundreds of significant experiences every day. A Yogi's inner experiences are the predominant experiences of his life, whereas for an ordinary person inner experiences are a very rare occurrence.

CHAPTER 3

SAMADHI AND BLISS:
THE INNER UNIVERSE

High, higher and highest is the plane of Delight. With our illumined consciousness, we rise into that plane and become self-enraptured. Having crossed the corridors of sublime silence and trance, we are now one with the Supreme.

— *Sri Chinmoy*

Question: Once you said that transcendental Delight is one of the divine qualities not manifested on earth. Why is that?

Sri Chinmoy: On the highest plane there is Existence-Consciousness-Bliss; we call it *Sat-Chit-Ananda. Sat* is Existence; *Chit* is Consciousness; *Ananda* is Delight. Consciousness is the source of everything, but Consciousness cannot stay without Delight and Existence. If there is no Existence, there can be no Consciousness. If there is Existence and Consciousness, Bliss is required for Self-fulfilment.

Great spiritual Masters from time immemorial have brought down the *Sat* and *Chit* aspects. But *Ananda* is much more difficult to bring down. Some could not bring it at all. Some brought it, but it lasted for only a few seconds or a few minutes and then went back up again. Peace is accessible; we can bring down Peace. Light and Power can easily be brought down. But the Delight which immortalises our inner and outer consciousness has not yet been established on earth. It comes and then goes away because it sees so much imperfection in the earth-atmosphere that it cannot remain.

Even spiritually advanced people are often confused. They feel an inner ecstasy which comes from the vital world, and they think this is the real Delight. But it is not so. Real Delight comes from the highest world to the soul, and from the soul it saturates the whole being.

This *Ananda* is absorbed differently from physical delight, or what we call pleasure or enjoyment. The supramental Delight is totally different from the world of pleasure and enjoyment. Once you get even an iota of it, you feel your entire inner being dancing for joy like a child with utmost purity, and your outer being feels true Immortality in its outer existence. If you get this Delight even for a second, you will remember it all your life.

All around us is the cosmic Game, the cosmic Play. The universe is full of joy, inner joy and outer joy. When realisation takes place, we have to feel the necessity of manifesting this constant Delight in our heart. This Delight glows, but does not actually burn. It has tremendous intensity, but it is all softness and absolutely sweet-flowing Nectar.

One day I brought it down into my gross physical, so that when I was smiling, at that time I was scattering the highest Delight to each of you. But I must say that it has all disappeared. There is nobody among the disciples who has kept any of it.

Question: Do children sometimes experience this kind of Delight?

Sri Chinmoy: No. Children do not have the highest Delight. They get psychic delight. They get some delight from the psychic being, from the inner being, or from the soul, which they express spontaneously. And very often children express their joy through their pure, uncorrupted vital. But the highest Delight, which comes from the plane of *Sat-Chit-Ananda*, children do not get. One can feel it only in one's deepest, highest meditation. Children also have to go through meditation, concentration and contemplation in order to experience this quality.

[*Sri Chinmoy then asked his disciples to try to invoke* Ananda]

Please place your right hand on your heart. Try to feel the most beautiful child on earth and in Heaven inside your heart. This is the soul. The men will naturally see the child as masculine, and the women will see the child as feminine. The soul is neither masculine nor feminine, but when it takes human incarnation, it takes a form. Try to see the child as only seven days old. In terms of spiritual evolution, some of you do not have even that seven-day-old child, forgive me to say. Although the souls started their journey millions of years ago, there are one or two individuals here who have had only one or two human incarnations. Naturally their souls' evolution is perhaps only a few hours old or a few minutes old in purely spiritual terms. Now, please think of the seven-day-old child. Then in absolute silence, please say *Ananda* seven times.

Question: Is there a difference between the realisation of one Master and the realisation of another?

Sri Chinmoy: As there are men and men, similarly there are Yogis and Yogis. Yogis are not all at the same level. A fully realised Yogi is he who is constantly one with God's Consciousness, constantly aware of his oneness with God. Again, there are half-realised or partially realised Yogis. A few hours of the day, when they are meditating, they will be one with God, and the rest of the time they will be like ordinary human beings. Their oneness with God depends on what kind of realisation the Yogis have achieved.

God-realisation is like a tree. One can run and touch the tree of realisation and say, "I have realised." But this realisation is only touching the foot of the tree. One is very happy in touching the foot of the tree, for he has seen that the fruit is there, the leaves and branches are there; he can touch them, hold them, feel them, and he knows that he has reached his goal. But another person will say, "No, I am not satisfied. I want to climb up a little and sit on a branch. Then I will feel that I have reached my goal." He goes one step higher, so naturally his realisation is superior. Again, there will be someone who will climb up to the topmost branch and eat the delicious fruit there. His realisation is higher still, because he has not only seen and touched the Highest, but has actually climbed up to the Highest. But he has no intention of coming down, because he feels that the moment he comes down he will again be an ordinary person and will be caught in the meshes of the ignorant world. He feels that once he climbs down, he will not be able to climb back up again.

But there is another type of realised soul who will not only climb up to the Highest for realisation, but will bring down the fruits of the tree for the world. He will come back for manifestation. He says, "I am not satisfied with sitting at the top of the tree. This is not my goal. What I have received I want to share with humanity." He has the capacity to climb up and climb down at his sweet will. When he climbs down, he brings down Compassion, Peace, Light and Bliss from above. And when he climbs up, he takes humanity with him. He places a few human beings on his shoulders and then climbs back up. He will keep those souls up there and come down again to take a few more up on his shoulders. His capacity is infinitely greater than that of the person who just comes and touches the tree. His realisation is the fullest.

In India, there have been quite a few spiritual Masters who were partially realised. They touched the foot of the tree, but did not climb up to the topmost branch. They are considered very great by the aspirants, but when you compare their standard with that of Sri Krishna or the Christ or the Buddha, you have to say that those who only touched the tree achieved only a partial realisation.

If a Hindu touches a drop of water from the Ganges, he will feel a sense of purity. But if somebody has the capacity to swim across the Ganges, naturally he will be more convinced that his entire body is purified. When it is a matter of realisation, also, one can be satisfied with a drop of nectar or one can say, "No, I need the boundless ocean." Again, one can say, "This boundless nectar is not only for me; it is for everybody. I want to share it with others." The realisation of the individual who actually has the capacity to share his highest realisation with others is undoubtedly superior to that of the other two.

Sri Ramakrishna used to speak about the *jivakoti* and the *ishvarakoti*. The *jivakoti* is one who has realised God but does not want to enter into the field of manifestation again. A person who has a raft, a tiny boat, can cross the sea of ignorance himself, but he cannot take others. But the *ishvarakoti*, who has a big ship, can accommodate hundreds and thousands of human souls and carry them across the sea of ignorance. He comes into the world again and again to liberate mankind.

Question: What is the lower samadhi?

Sri Chinmoy: There are various minor samadhis, and among the minor samadhis, *savikalpa* samadhi happens to be the highest. Right after *savikalpa* comes *nirvikalpa* samadhi, but there is a great yawning gulf between *savikalpa* and *nirvikalpa*. However, even though *savikalpa* samadhi is one step below *nirvikalpa,* we do not use the term 'lower'. We do not call *savikalpa* samadhi lower than *nirvikalpa*; they are two radically different samadhis. Again, there is something even beyond *nirvikalpa* samadhi called *sahaja* samadhi. But *savikalpa* and *nirvikalpa* samadhi are the most well-known samadhis.

In *savikalpa* samadhi, for a short period of time you lose all human consciousness. In this state the conception of time and space is altogether different. With the human time you cannot judge; with the human way of looking at space you cannot judge. In that samadhi, for an hour or two hours you are completely in another world. You see there that almost everything is done. Here in this world there are many desires still unfulfilled in yourself and in others. Millions of desires are not fulfilled, and millions of things remain to be done. But when you are in *savikalpi* samadhi, you see that practically everything is done; you have nothing to do. You are only an instrument. If you are used, well and good; otherwise, things are all done. But from *savikalpi* samadhi everybody has to return to ordinary consciousness.

Even in *savikalpa* samadhi there are grades. Just as there are brilliant students and poor students in the same class in school, so also in *savikalpa* samadhi some aspirants reach the highest grade, while less aspiring seekers reach a lower or a middle rung of the ladder, where everything is not so clear and vivid as on the highest level.

In *savikalpa* samadhi there are thoughts and ideas coming from various angles, but they do not affect you. While you are meditating, you remain unperturbed, and your inner being functions in a dynamic and confident manner. But when you are a little higher, when you have become one with the soul in *nirvikalpa* samadhi, there will be no ideas or thoughts at all. Here nature's dance stops. There is no nature, only infinite Peace and Bliss. The Knower and the Known have become one. Everything is tranquil. Here you enjoy a supremely divine, all-pervading, self-amorous ecstasy. You become the object of enjoyment, you become the enjoyer and you become the enjoyment itself.

Nirvikalpa samadhi is the highest samadhi that most spiritual Masters attain, and then only if they have achieved realisation. It lasts for a few hours or a few days, and then one has to come down. When one comes down, what happens? Very often one forgets his own name. One forgets his own age. He cannot speak properly. But through continued practice, gradually one becomes able to come down from *nirvikalpa* samadhi and immediately function in a normal way.

There were spiritual Masters in the hoary past who attained *nirvikalpa* samadhi and did not come down. They maintained their highest samadhi and found it impossible to enter into the world atmosphere and work like human beings. One cannot operate in the world while in that state of consciousness; it is simply impossible.

Generally, when one enters into *nirvikalpa* samadhi, one does not want to come back into the world again. If one stays there for eighteen or twenty-one days, there is every possibility that he will leave the body. But there is a divine dispensation. If the Supreme wants a particular soul to work here on earth, even after twenty-one or twenty-two days, the Supreme takes the individual into another channel of dynamic, divine consciousness and has him return to the earth-plane to act.

Sahaja samadhi is by far the highest type of samadhi. In this samadhi one is in the highest consciousness, but at the same time he is working in the gross physical world. One maintains the experience of *nirvikalpa* samadhi while simultaneously entering into earthly activities. One has become the soul and at the same time is utilising the body as a perfect instrument. In *sahaja* samadhi one walks like an ordinary human being. One eats. One does the usual things that an ordinary human being does. But in the inmost recesses of his heart he is surcharged with divine illumination. When one has this *sahaja* samadhi, one becomes the Lord and Master of Reality. One can go at his sweet will to the Highest and then come down to the earth-consciousness to manifest.

After achieving the highest type of realisation, on very rare occasions one is blessed with *sahaja* samadhi. Very few spiritual Masters have achieved this state — only one or two. For *sahaja* samadhi, the Supreme's infinite Grace is required, or one has to be very powerful and lucky. *Sahaja* samadhi comes only when one has established inseparable oneness with the Supreme, or when one wants to show, on rare occasions, that he *is* the Supreme. He who has achieved *sahaja* samadhi and remains in this samadhi, consciously and perfectly manifests God at every second, and is thus the greatest pride of the transcendental Supreme.

Question: Is the turiya *consciousness a form of samadhi? Is it in any way related to* sahaja *samadhi?*

Sri Chinmoy: The *turiya* consciousness is the transcendental Reality. It is not a form of samadhi in the accurate sense of the term. When an individual soul establishes permanent and constant union with the Supreme Being, we say that he is enjoying the *turiya* consciousness. The possessor of *turiya* consciousness usually does not come down for manifestation because he likes to remain immersed in *Sat-Chit-Ananda*, Existence-Consciousness-Bliss. Here the seeker reaches the absolute height of evolution. This loftiest realisation has no direct link with *sahaja* samadhi.

Sahaja samadhi holds the *turiya* consciousness. A possessor of *sahaja* samadhi embodies the *turiya* consciousness, and it is he who challenges earth-ignorance with a view to transforming it into the perfect creation. He embodies the highest transcendental Truth, Light, Peace, Bliss, Power and all divine qualities in boundless measure in his being, and he manifests these divine qualities in the easiest and most effective way in his multifarious day-to-day activities. In his outer life he acts like a divine child who has Eternity's Height and Infinity's Light at his disposal, sharing them with aspiring humanity cheerfully and unreservedly.

Question: Could you speak a little more extensively about the experience of nirvikalpa *samadhi?*

Sri Chinmoy: Nirvikalpa samadhi cannot be explained by any individual, no matter how great he is. It is an experience which can be understood only by trying to identify and become one with someone who has attained the experience. We must try to enter into the experience rather than ask the experience to come to our level. When we enter into *nirvikalpa* samadhi, the experience itself is the reality. But when we want to tell others, to put it into words, we have to come down very far and use the mind; we have to couch the experience in human concepts. Therefore, the consciousness of *nirvikalpa* samadhi can never be adequately explained or expressed. The revelation of the experience can never be like the original experience.

I am trying my best to tell you about this from a very high consciousness, but still my mind is subtly expressing it. In *nirvikalpa* samadhi we have no mind. We see the Creator, the Creation and the Observer as one Person. There the object of adoration and the person who is adoring become totally one; the Lover and the Beloved become totally one. We go beyond everything, and at the same time we see that everything is real. Here in the ordinary world I will say you are unreal and you will say I am unreal because of our different opinions. But in *nirvikalpa* samadhi we go beyond all differences; there the mind does not function at all.

When we enter into *nirvikalpa* samadhi, the first thing we feel is that our heart is larger than the universe itself. Now we see the world around us, and the universe seems infinitely larger than we are. But this is because the world and the universe are now perceived by the limited mind. When we are in *nirvikalpa* samadhi, we see the universe like a tiny dot inside our vast heart.

In *nirvikalpa* samadhi there is infinite Bliss. There is nothing in comparison to the quantity, not to speak of the quality, of that Bliss. Bliss is a vague word to most of us. We hear that there is something called Bliss, and some people say they have experienced it, but most of us have no firsthand knowledge of it. When we enter into *nirvikalpa* samadhi, however, we not only feel Bliss, but we grow into that Bliss.

The third thing we feel in *nirvikalpa* samadhi is Power. All the power that all the occultists have put together is nothing compared with the Power we have in *nirvikalpa* samadhi. But the power that we can take from samadhi to utilise on earth is infinitesimal compared with the entirety. It is like what we require to blink our eye. All this I am expressing through the mind; it is not exact. But I cannot express with words more of the truth that I have realised.

I wish to say only that to enter into any level of samadhi is infinitely easier than to transform the human consciousness into the divine consciousness. That I have been trying to do, you have been trying to do, the Supreme has been trying to do. All of us here are trying for only one thing, and that is the transformation of human nature— physical, vital, mental and psychic. When that is done, perfect Perfection will dawn both here on earth and there in Heaven.

How can this transformation take place? Through aspiration. The world has to aspire, creation has to aspire, and only then can the spiritual Masters bring down Heaven onto earth. Heaven, as we say, is a state of consciousness. In samadhi, all is Heaven, all is Bliss, Light, Peace. But when we come down into the world again, all is suffering, darkness, fear, worry. How can we make a conscious connection between this world of ours and the highest state of samadhi? Through constant aspiration. There is no other medicine but constant aspiration, not for a day or two, but for a whole lifetime. To realise God takes many, many incarnations. But when you have a fully realised spiritual Master, it becomes much easier. It may take you one incarnation, or two, or three or four. Otherwise, for a normal human being it takes many, many hundreds of incarnations, even to attain the higher experiences or so-called minor realisations. But a realised Master knows the souls and stays in the souls. Since he can do this, it is easy for him to deal with each aspirant according to his soul's necessity, for his soul's development and fulfilment.

Question: What is the difference between samadhi and God-realisation?

Sri Chinmoy: Samadhi is a realm of consciousness. Many people have entered into samadhi, but realisation comes only when we have become one with the highest Absolute. We can enter into some samadhis without realising the Highest.

Entering samadhi is like knowing the alphabet, but realisation is like having a Ph.D. There is no comparison between samadhi and realisation. Samadhi is a state of consciousness in which one can stay for a few hours or a few days. After twenty-one days usually the body does not function. But once one has achieved realisation, it lasts forever. And in realisation, one's whole consciousness has become inseparably and eternally one with God.

There are three stages of samadhi: *savikalpa* samadhi, *nirvikalpa* samadhi and *sahaja* samadhi. *Savikalpa* samadhi is an exalted and glowing state of consciousness, whereas realisation is a conscious, natural and manifesting state of consciousness. When realisation dawns, the seeker enjoys freedom from the human personality and human individuality. He is like a tiny drop of water which enters into the ocean. Once it enters, it becomes the ocean. At that time, we do not see the personality or the individuality of the one drop. When one realises the highest Truth, the finite in him enters into the Infinite and realises and achieves the Infinite as its very own. Once realisation has taken place, a Master can easily enter into *savikalpa* samadhi. *Nirvikalpa* samadhi, too, is not difficult for a God-realised soul to attain. Only *sahaja* samadhi, which is the highest type of samadhi, is a problem, even for the very highest God-realised souls.

Question: In the highest state of samadhi, when you look at other human beings, what kind of consciousness do you feel in them?

Sri Chinmoy: When one is in the highest transcendental samadhi, the physical personality of others disappears. We do not see others as human beings. We see only a flow of consciousness, like a river that is entering into the ocean. He who is in the highest trance becomes the ocean, and he who is in a lower state of consciousness is the river. The river flows into the sea and becomes one with the sea. The one who is enjoying the highest samadhi does not notice any individuality or personality in the others. A human being who is not in this state of samadhi is a flowing river of consciousness, while the one who is in samadhi has become the sea itself, the sea of Peace and Light.

Question: For how long can a realised soul remain in savikalpa *samadhi?*

Sri Chinmoy: One need not be a realised soul in order to enter into *savikalpa* samadhi. If someone is a great aspirant and if he has been meditating for many years, he can have *savikalpa* samadhi. It is not that difficult. *Savikalpa* samadhi can last for several hours. When Sri Ramakrishna used to touch seekers and give them a kind of trance and samadhi, it was for a few hours. In *savikalpa* samadhi one does not stay more than a day or two, because it is not necessary and not advisable. Only *nirvikalpa* samadhi goes on for seven, eight, nine, ten days, because *nirvikalpa* samadhi is more important in terms of our inner life.

For a spiritually realised person there is no definite boundary to his *savikalpa* samadhi. At his will he can come and go. At any moment he can enter, and he can stay a few hours or days. Certainly it is not an easy thing for an aspirant to do, but it is not the most difficult thing for a Yogi. If someone is a realised soul, if he is a real Yogi or spiritual Master or Avatar, for him *savikalpa* samadhi is just like playing with toys. In his case it is very simple, but for an ordinary aspirant, certainly it is difficult.

Question: I understand that a liberated soul can prolong his stay in the physical world for twelve or fifteen days even while he is in nirvikalpa *samadhi.*

Sri Chinmoy: A liberated soul can safely stay for twenty-one or twenty-two days in *nirvikalpa* samadhi if the Divine wants that particular soul to continue on the path of dynamic manifestation. If the Divine wants the individual to remain in the Brahman of static realisation, then his soul will not return to the earth-consciousness after he has attained *nirvikalpa* samadhi and he will have to leave the body. But if the Divine wants, after eleven, twelve or thirteen days, He will say: "I want you to work for Me in the world. You must go back."

The name of the plane from which the Masters come back is the Supermind. This is where the actual creation starts. Higher than this is the level of *Sat-Chit-Ananda:* Existence-Consciousness-Bliss. The spiritual Masters who want divine manifestation here on earth are trying to manifest first the Supermind, which is the golden Consciousness from which the creation descended. When that is manifested, the spiritual Masters who are here to bring down the highest Consciousness will then bring down *Sat-Chit-Ananda.* These three qualities can never be separated. They have to come together here on earth. The Supreme wants the whole divine manifestation to take place here on earth, not in Heaven or anywhere else.

In our Indian scriptures it is said that man is greater than the cosmic gods because the cosmic gods are satisfied with the Bliss of Heaven, whereas man is not satisfied until he actually achieves liberation. If the cosmic gods want to make progress, if they want liberation or manifestation, even they have to take human form and come to earth. Manifestation cannot take place anywhere else. In India there are thousands of gods, and we appreciate, we admire, we adore them because right now they are superior to us. When we suffer from a headache, if we soulfully invoke a god, then he will come and take it away. But the cosmic gods can do nothing further than that. When man realises God, at that time these cosmic gods are of no help to him. At that time man is superior, because he is attaining constant and conscious union with the absolute Supreme.

Question: Will a Master know before-hand if he is to leave the body during samadhi?

Sri Chinmoy: Yes, he will know. Even an ordinary man often knows when he is going to leave the body. Sometimes his departed relatives will appear and say, "Come, my friend, now it is your time to follow us. How long we have waited for you! It is time to take birth here, to enjoy Heaven." They want to celebrate his arrival. Here on earth we die, but there in Heaven we are born to all our departed dear ones.

Question: Could you explain the difference between samadhi of the heart and nirvikalpa *samadhi?*

Sri Chinmoy: These are two different things. In the heart centre you do not get *nirvikalpa* samadhi. *Nirvikalpa* samadhi you get only when you go beyond the domain of the mind—far beyond, to the very highest level of consciousness. When you go inside the heart, deep, deeper, deepest, there you get the feeling of inseparable oneness with your Inner Pilot, the Supreme. So these are two different things.

Question: Is there anything higher than nirvikalpa *samadhi?*

Sri Chinmoy: Nirvikalpa samadhi and other samadhis are all high stages. But there is a stage which is superior to *nirvikalpa* samadhi. That is the stage of divine transformation, absolute transformation. You can be in samadhi, but samadhi does not give you transformation. While you are in your trance you become exalted, for you are one with God. But when you come back into the material plane, you become an ordinary man. But if you have transformed your outer and inner consciousness, then you are no more affected by the ignorance of the world.

Question: If a Master is in sahaja *samadhi all the time, which is the highest form of samadhi, is it a sort of conscious descent when he goes into* nirvikalpa *samadhi?*

Sri Chinmoy: It is not like that. *Sahaja* samadhi encompasses the other samadhis— *savikalpa* and *nirvikalpa*—and it goes beyond, beyond. Samadhi is like a big building with many floors. When one is in

sahaja samadhi, he is the owner of the whole
building. He has the height of *nirvikalpa*,
and the heights far above that, and at the
same time he has achieved the perfection,
wealth and capacity of all the other floors.
On the one hand he has encompassed within
himself all the floors, and on the other hand
he is above them. *Nirvikalpa* is like one
height, say the thirtieth floor; it is very high,
but it has only its own limited capacity. It
cannot bring any of its capacity to the
basement. If one has *nirvikapla*, he is afraid
to go down into the basement, because he
may not be able to go back up again. But
sahaja consciousness is above the thirtieth
floor and, at the same time, it can be in the
basement also. *Sahaja* samadhi will not be
satisfied with thirtieth floor; it will be
satisfied only when it touches the basement,
the first floor, the second floor, all the
floors. The power of *sahaja* samadhi is such
that it can take one to any floor.

Right now, for example, I am talking
with you people. You can say that I am on
the lowest floor. Not in terms of consciousness or achievement, but in terms of height,
that is my actual location. But if I own the
building, if my consciousness has captured
the entire building, then I can be anywhere.

When it is a matter of actual location, I may be in the basement; but when it is a matter of possession, I have earned, I have achieved and I constantly have all the floors as my own.

Question: If a Master is in sahaja *samadhi all the time, does that mean* nirvikalpa *samadhi is not fulfilling to him?*

Sri Chinmoy: If one is in *sahaja* samadhi, in one sense nothing can fulfil him because he is already fulfilled in his inner life. As an individual, he has gone beyond fulfilment. When one is in *sahaja* samadhi, there is nothing more for him to achieve or learn. The Master may not be a carpenter, but he has such oneness with the universe that he can identify with a carpenter and make himself feel in his own living consciousness that he *is* that carpenter. At that time, the Master's being and the carpenter's whole being are totally one.

But when it is a matter of the fulfilment of everyone within the Master—fulfilment in him and for the Supreme—that is not yet done. When it is a matter of manifestation, he is stuck. In that he is not fulfilled. My own personal realisation I achieved long, long ago. But when it is a matter of the fulfilment of those whom I call my own, in that I am not yet fulfilled. In the outer life, in the manifestation, I will be fulfilled only when you are fulfilled, when he is fulfilled, when she is fulfilled. If somebody leads a better life, if somebody prays for five minutes most soulfully, that is my fulfilment. If you pray most sincerely, one minute more than you did yesterday, that is my real fulfilment, because of my oneness with you.

Question: When you bring down Peace and Light to us, do you have to go into nirvikalpa *samadhi?*

Sri Chinmoy: No, I do not have to go to any particular state of consciousness to give you something. All spiritual qualities are inside me, in the spiritual heart. The spiritual heart is infinitely larger than the universe itself. The whole universe is inside the spiritual heart. When I want to offer Light I may look up, and you may think that I have gone very high, beyond the heart. But the heart is like a globe which encompasses the whole universe. Inside the heart is the plane for love, the plane for light, the plane for peace. Each plane is like a different house. Some planes have a little of everything, and some planes are specialised. But all are inside the heart, which is where a spiritual Master lives, and from there he brings everything.

One has to develop the spiritual heart. Everybody does not have the same capacity. Everybody has potentiality, but it must be developed. It is not like our oneness with God, which is something we all possess equally but have misplaced. No, the capacity of the spiritual heart is something we actually have to achieve in the process of evolution. Gradually it grows from a seed to a plant to a huge banyan tree, as our oneness with God increases. With unconscious oneness we enter into the world. Through the process of prayer, meditation, love, devotion and surrender, we develop conscious oneness. The heart develops from the consciousness of a child to the consciousness of the eldest member of the family, who knows everything that the father knows. When we have developed the spiritual heart, at that time we come to realise our identity with the Mother and Father of the universe.

Question: Do you teach your disciples any specific technique for attaining samadhi?

Sri Chinmoy: No. Samadhi is a very high state of consciousness. If the beginner comes to kindergarten and asks the teacher how he can study for his Master's degree, the teacher will simply laugh. He will say, "How can I tell you?" Before we are ready to try to attain samadhi, we have to go through many, many, many inner spiritual experiences. Then there comes a time when the Master sees that the student is ready to enter into *savikalpa* samadhi. *Nirvikalpa* samadhi is out of the question for seekers right now. One has to be a most advanced seeker before he can think of attaining *nirvikalpa* samadhi. But before that, *savikalpa* samadhi is enough. If one gets *savikalpa* samadhi, it is more than enough for quite a number of years, even for this lifetime.

Nirvikalpa samadhi one gets only in the highest stage of his aspiration. Unfortunately, I do not have anyone among my disciples now whom I can help to enter into that state. I am very proud of my disciples. They are very sincere, very devoted, and they are making very fast proress; but the time has not come for them to enter into *nirvikalpa* samadhi. For all seekers I wish to say that the spiritual ladder has quite a few rungs. We have to climb up one step at a time. *Nirvikalpa* samadhi, for my disciples at least, is a far cry right now.

Question: As you evolve spiritually, does your meditation become longer, and does it change its focus or orientation?

Sri Chinmoy: A person who is highly developed spiritually will naturally be able to meditate for a longer time than a relative beginner. But meditation is not a matter of time, but a matter of aspiration. If one has true aspiration, deep aspiration, one will be able to meditate for a longer time, because meditation will be easy for him. He will feel that to realise God is the only objective in his life. Someone with just a little aspiration will meditate for five or ten minutes as a discipline or an obligation, but with little joy or inspiration.

Many people believe that a true seeker must meditate at least eight hours a day. I did it. Even though I attained realisation in my past incarnation, when I was thirteen years old in this incarnation I was meditating for eight, nine, ten, thirteen hours a day. But I had the capacity. I don't advise my disciples to do this, because I know the capacity of my children. They would have a mental breakdown. It would be simply impossible for them. It would not be true meditation. It is not that I am saying that they are insincere. No! They are most sincere. But capacity is like a muscle. One has to develop it gradually. You start with fifteen minutes and then go on to half an hour. Those who are now meditating for half an hour will soon be able to meditate for an hour or an hour and a half.

Gradually, gradually, your inner capacity will grow. At the proper time, your inner being will tell you or I will tell you when you can meditate for eight hours. But right now, do not even try. It will simply create a disaster in your life.

After one has achieved realisation, it is not necessary for him to meditate the way an aspirant or a seeker meditates. When one has attained realisation, which is oneness with the Supreme, his meditation is continually going on—in this world, in that world, in all the worlds. When one has realised God, he does not meditate to achieve something or to go beyond something. He meditates to bring down peace, light and bliss into humanity or to awaken the consciousness of his disciples.

Question: If meditation gives you such a marvellous feeling, why don't you stay in your highest meditation twenty-four hours a day? Why do you come here and give a lecture, for example?

Sri Chinmoy: What does one do when he has studied for quite a few years and has received his Master's degree? He starts teaching. In my case, my eternal Father has given me a big heart. I know how I suffered to realise Him; I know what kind of pangs and agonies I went through to realise the Highest. Now I am seeing these pangs in my brothers and sisters. They are suffering as I did. Once up a time, I, too, was wallowing in the pleasures of ignorance. Now I see that same thing happening to them. Since God, out of His infinite Bounty, gave me Love, Light and other divine qualities, let me offer them to that part of suffering humanity which is crying for them. I am not for the entire world. I am only for those who really want Light from me. If God wants me to be of service to my brothers and sisters who really need light, then by serving humanity I am pleasing God.

A God-realised soul is he who wants to please God in God's own way. Since God wants me to be of service to aspiring human beings, then that is what gives me greatest joy, and not staying in my highest consciousness, which I could easily do. Very often I show that consciousness to my disciples and students during our meditations. They have seen it often. But if I stay in that consciousness all the time, who will derive any benefit from me? I will be acting like a selfish fellow. I have the wealth, but if I keep it all for myself, then what good is it to the poverty-stricken world? If I use it for others who are desperately in need of it, only then will God be pleased with me. These people need God, and God also needs them. I am the intermediary. I go to God with folded hands because He has something to offer. I take what He has and with folded hands I offer it to mankind. Mankind also has something to offer. Its offering is ignorance. I just exchange God's offering, Light, for man's offering, ignorance.

The real work, if there be any, of a Guru is to show the world that his deeds are in perfect harmony with his teachings.

— *Sri Chinmoy*

CHAPTER 4

THE ILLUMINED MASTER:
MESSENGER FROM THE BEYOND

The Guru is not the body. The Guru is the revelation and manifestation of a divine Power upon earth.

— *Sri Chinmoy*

Question: Is a liberated soul the same as a spiritual Master who tries to help humanity?

Sri Chinmoy: The world has seen thousands and thousands of liberated souls, but not all liberated souls work in the world of ignorance. Many are afraid that ignorance will threaten them and try to devour them. One who is just liberated has come out of the room which is full of darkness, but this does not necessarily mean he is truly qualified to be a spiritual guide. To be a spiritual guide in the highest sense of the term, one must be commissioned by the Supreme. One may have spiritual knowledge, spiritual power and so forth, but if he is not authorised by the Highest to guide humanity, he cannot be a real spiritual Master.

Question: Does every person who realises God become a spiritual Master?

Sri Chinmoy: There are hundreds of students every year who get their Master's degree from a university. Some then enter into an office or business, while others begin to teach. Similarly, in the spiritual life, some people who have realised God teach others how to realise God, and some do not. Those who do not teach in the world are God-realised nevertheless. We cannot deny it. But it has taken them many incarnations to cross the barriers of ignorance, and they are now really tired. It is not an easy thing to realise God, and they feel they have acted like real divine heroes in the battlefield of life. They have fought against fear, doubt, anxieties, worries, imperfections, limitations and bondage and conquered these forces. Now they feel that they have every right to withdraw from the battlefield and take rest. These souls speak to God, and if God says they do not have to take conscious part in the cosmic Game any more, and may just observe, then they withdraw. If they have God's permission, naturally they can remain passive.

But the souls who do not take part in God's manifestation are also doing something very great. They may not take an active part in the world, they may not go from one place to another to teach or open spiritual centres and accept disciples, but in their meditation they try to offer illumination inwardly by offering their conscious good will to mankind. How many people offer their good will to mankind? Ordinary human beings quarrel, fight and consciously or unconsciously do many undivine things against God's Will. But in the case of these realised souls, they do not enter into any kind of conflict with God's Will; their will has become one with God's Will.

We cannot say that he who works outwardly for mankind is greater than he who helps inwardly. What is of paramount importance is to listen to God's Will. We cannot say that one who is crying for mankind and trying to help is greater than one who withdraws. He alone is great who listens to God's Will. If God tells one illumined soul, "I do not need you to move around from place to place. You just give your Light inwardly," then that person is great by offering his Light inwardly. And if God tells another soul, "I want you to go into the world and offer humanity the Light you have," then that Master is great by helping humanity. Everything depends on what God wants from a particular soul.

Question: If someone has realised God, why would he want to leave the higher Bliss and come down into the darkness of the earth to help others?

Sri Chinmoy: There are some spiritual Masters who do not care for the manifestation of their inner Divinity or, you can say, for the manifestation of God's Divinity on earth. They do not care for the transformation of the earth-consciousness. They say to the world, "If I try to help you, your doubts, fears, anxieties, worries, limitations and bondages will all enter into me. I worked hard for my own realisation, so the best thing is for you also to work hard for *your* realisation. If you work hard, God will never deny you the fruits."

Again, there are some spiritual Masters who *do* care for the illumination of the earth-consciousness. They see that they are eating most delicious food or drinking nectar in the inner world, while their brothers are deprived of it. This kind of Master identifies with humanity and feels it is his business to awaken the consciousness of his fellow human beings, his slumbering brothers. If there are people on earth who are covered by ignorance and are wasting their time in idleness when they really need nourishment, this Master feels sorry. He feels sorry that these people still want to remain in ignorance when they could easily go beyond the boundaries of ignorance. Since a spiritual Master has himself experienced all kinds of suffering, he does not consider his fellow human beings objects of pity. He identifies himself totally with them. He has realised God, but he feels that unless and until everybody is realised, he himself is imperfect and incomplete. When it is a matter of personal need, the Master does not need anything more from God, but he becomes part and parcel of humanity out of his Compassion.

He says, "I shall play the role of a father." In a family we see that the father works very, very hard and amasses some wealth, and then his children do not have to work so hard. He gives all kinds of material help to his children, and they get the benefit of his labour. When a real spiritual Master comes into the world, he has worked very, very hard to realise the Truth, and he possesses boundless Peace, Light and Bliss in his inner life. He offers this wealth to his spiritual children, because they claim him as their very own and he claims them. Those who have established total oneness with the Master and who try to fulfil the Master according to their capacity, those who become extremely close to their Master, receive what the Master has and is. Their realisation is entirely up to the Master. It is like the case of the father who has millions of dollars. The son has pleased the father, so the father gives the son his wealth.

Again, the father will always see whether the son is capable of receiving the money and utilising it in a proper way. If the father sees that the son is going to utilise the money properly, naturally he gives the son money. But if the father sees that the son will squander ten dollars rather than use it for a divine purpose, then naturally he will not lavish his money on this worthless son. In the spiritual world it is also like that. If one is really sincere, if one feels that he can exist without everything, but not without God, then it is possible for him to realise God in one incarnation with the help of a spiritual Master, because he will properly utilise what the Master gives him.

Question: Won't a person lose his realisation if he comes down from the realisation-tree and has to face the darkness and ignorance of the world?

Sri Chinmoy: If you are afraid that a realised soul will lose his divinity and realisation if he mixes with ordinary people, then you are mistaken. When you realise God, God gives you more power than He has given His unrealised children. Spiritual Masters have a free access to God's Omnipotence and to all His other qualities. If spiritual Masters did not have more power than their disciples, who still suffer from fear, doubt, anxiety and other undivine qualities, they would never mix with them or even accept them. They would know that they would be devoured, totally devoured by their disciples' imperfections. But they are not afraid, because they know that their realisation has much more power than any negative forces in their disciples. Before realisation, even up to the very last hour, it is possible to fall from the realisation-tree. But once you have realised God, you have won the race. This victory is permanent and eternal. Nothing and no one can take it away from you, nor can you lose it.

Question: Does a realised Master who chooses to help suffering humanity lose anything by doing so, especially since humanity is so reluctant to accept his wealth?

Sri Chinmoy: No! He is like someone who knows how to climb a tree well. He has the capacity to climb up and climb down. When the Master climbs down, he does not lose anything because he knows that at the next moment he will be able to climb up again. Suppose a child at the foot of the tree says, "Please give me a fruit; please give me a most delicious mango." Immediately the Master will bring one down and then he will climb up again. And if nobody else asks for a mango, he will sit on the branch and wait.

Here on earth, if one human being has something to offer and the other person does not take it, then the first person gets furious. He says, "You fool! It is for your own good that I am giving it." He will scold the other person and be very displeased if his offering is not accepted. In the case of a spiritual Master, it is different. He will come with his wealth, but if humanity does not accept it, he will not curse humanity. Even if humanity insults him and speaks ill of him, he will not lodge a complaint against humanity to God. With his boundless patience he will say, "All right, today you are sleeping. Perhaps tomorrow you will get up and see what I have to offer. I will wait for you." If you are fast asleep and someone pinches you and shouts, "Get up! Get up!" he is not doing you a favour. You will be annoyed. But the spiritual Master will not bother you; he will not ask you to get up. He will stay beside your bed and wait until you get up, and the moment you get up he will ask you to look at the sun.

If he is a real spiritual Master, he will not lose anything if earth rejects what he has, because he is well established in his inner life, in his inner consciousness. Again, if humanity accepts what he offers, he does not lose anything, either. The more he gives, the more he gets from the Source. Just as in the ordinary life the more knowledge we offer to others, the more we get, in the spiritual life also it is the same. A spiritual Master will never run short of Peace, Light and Bliss, because he is connected with the infinite Source of all.

Ordinary aspirants or the so-called Masters have limited capacity. If they give away something, they cannot replace it. But when one is in touch with unlimited capacity in the inner world, his source is like an ocean. One cannot empty the infinite inner ocean. The real Master wants to give everything to his devoted disciples, but their power of receptivity is limited. So he tries to widen their vessels and make them as big as possible so that the disciples can receive the Peace, Light and Bliss that he brings for them. But he cannot force an aspirant to receive more than he has the capacity to hold. If he does, then the vessel will give way. So a Master can only pour and pour and pour his infinite Light into his disciples, but once the limit of their receptivity is reached, it will all be wasted on them.

Question: When a Master brings down more light, peace and bliss than those meditating with him can absorb, what happens to it?

Sri Chinmoy: It is not all lost. It is scattered over the earth. It enters into the earth-atmosphere and becomes the earth's possession. When spiritual Masters bring down divine qualities from above, Mother Earth embodies them as her own. Then, when someone in the street or elsewhere aspires, he will get this peace and light from the earth-consciousness, but he will not know where it is coming from.

Question: I once read that a Master will come down to help humanity in this world, and then he will continue helping from other worlds. Is this true?

Sri Chinmoy: Whenever there is a necessity, great spiritual Masters come down to help the yet-unrealised souls. They are playing their part in God's Game, His divine *Lila.* Seekers get a tremendous opportunity when they are helped in their aspiration by real spiritual Masters, for by personal effort, without the help of a Master, it is very, very difficult to get realisation. Aspiration is of paramount importance, but mere aspiration cannot give realisation. There is a necessity for the divine Grace. And this Grace comes most easily through the intervention of Avatars, Yogis, saints and sages. The world is progressing and evolving as quickly as it is just because great spiritual Masters are coming into the world to help.

After working on earth for a few incarnations, the Master may want to continue his work for humanity from the other world. At that time, he knows all the hidden corners of the Mother Earth; he knows every heartbeat of the earth-consciousness, so he is able to work from outside.

Question: Why is it so difficult for a realised Master to be accepted by the world?

Sri Chinmoy: The world is not ready for spiritual Masters. They come into the world out of their infinite Compassion. When they leave, some Masters promise that they will come back as long as there are people still unrealised on earth. They are sincere when they say this, but when they go up to the higher worlds and see earth's ingratitude, they change their minds. They ask themselves why they should waste their precious time if humanity is sleeping, and why they should come back just to be kicked by an ungrateful humanity.

Humanity needs spiritual Masters for awakening and illumination, but in the outer life people do not feel any urgency.

The world is not ready, and perhaps it will never be ready as a whole. When the Masters come, they find unwilling, unaspiring human beings. For spiritual Masters to realise God, it takes quite a few incarnations. Realisation is such an arduous task to perform. But it is much more difficult to manifest God on earth. That is why many spiritual Masters do not come down for manifestation.

Although God is inside each human being, unfortunately the animal still predominates in man. When the Masters are dealing with humanity, they see it is all animality. Look at the example of Sri Ramakrishna. He took so many negative and undivine forces from his disciples; he suffered so much from their poison. Otherwise, for such a pure man to be afflicted with malignant cancer would have been impossible.

To realise God is difficult. And after realisation, to live in the ignorant world and stay with humanity is more difficult. But to remain in the consciousness of the Highest while working in the lowest, and to bring down the highest Light into the lowest and make the lowest receive and accept it, is most difficult. Again, when we say something is difficult or most difficult, we are only belittling ourselves. After all, what are spiritual Masters? They are God's chosen children. God's chosen children are identified with God all the time through Eternity. God can never be separated from His children, His creation. So nothing is difficult if we see it from the highest absolute point of view: neither to realise God nor to serve God in humanity, nor to take responsibility for bringing humanity to Divinity or Divinity to humanity. Everything is easy, easier, easiest, if there is something called God-touch. If God's Will touches some action, then it is very easy.

Question: Among those Masters who decide, after realisation, to go out into the world to help humanity, why do some accept large numbers of disciples while others do not?

Sri Chinmoy: Sometimes the Supreme makes the decision, but He does not impose His Will. There are some Masters who, after having their major realisation, are asked by the Supreme, "What is your will? What do you want to do?" If the Master says, "I want to work for so many people, I want to do this much work," then the Supreme says, "All right, granted, with My Blessings." Then there are some who do not make any hard and fast rule as to how far they want to go. They say, "I will try my best up to the end. I need Your Blessings. I need Your Grace. I will try to manifest as much as possible. I set no limits."

With some Masters, there is a limit to the number of disciples they want. With others, there is no end to their aspiration to serve. They remain an open channel and tell the Supreme that they will try their best to fulfil Him and manifest Him until the end of their lives. And not only that, but after leaving the body also, they promise to try to continue His work through their disciples. So it depends on the individual Master and how much spiritual responsibility he wants to accept.

Regarding the number of disciples a Master may have, this depends on what kind of people he accepts. If he is very selective and wants only souls that are fully dedicated, intensely aspiring and absolutely destined for the spiritual life, then he will accept only a handful. Sri Ramakrishna, for example, wanted only a limited number of disciples. He was very particular about his disciples. But some Yogis say, "Anyone who wants to learn anything about the spiritual life is welcome to my community." Again, some spiritual Masters say, "Let everyone progress according to his own standard." So they accept thousands of disciples.

True spiritual Masters will only accept disciples who are meant for them. If I know that somebody will make faster progress through some other Master, then occultly and spiritually I will make that person feel in a few months' time that he is not meant for me. What matters is not the number of disciples a Master has, but whether he takes them to the Goal. If I am realised and somebody else is realised, we are like two brothers with one common Father. Our goal is to take our younger brothers and sisters, humanity, to the Father. The game will be complete only when all people are taken to God. If two Masters are real brothers from the same Father, then how can one Master be unhappy or displeased if somebody goes to the Supreme through the other Master? In the spiritual life we always go together. It is not who has done it, but whether the thing is done. Who has done it is only name and form, which will be obliterated in history. What matters is that evolution has taken place on earth.

Question: Why do some spiritual Masters go out into the world to increase their following?

Sri Chinmoy: A true Master is not interested in the number of his devotees, since by God's Grace the Master and the aspirant are bound to find each other. But Sri Ramakrishna used to go up to the top floor of his house and cry for spiritual disciples. He used to ask Mother Kali why the disciples he was destined to have did not come to him. Now, people may ask why he could not wait for God's Hour. But the thing is that God's Hour had come for Sri Ramakrishna, but the ignorance of the world was blocking its path. God told him to do something and gave him the capacity, but ignorance was standing right in front of him and delaying, delaying, delaying his manifestation. Sri Ramakrishna · was not crying for disciples who would come and touch his feet. He was crying for disciples who would be his real arms and hands, who would fly with him into the universal Consciousness, who would work for him, and in that way work for God.

Nobody is indispensable, true. But, at the same time, each person *is* indispensable so long as he is absolutely sincere in his aspiration and in his service to the Mission of the Supreme. Out of pride and vanity, nobody can feel that he is necessary; but everybody is necessary when he is a sincere, dedicated chosen instrument of God. The Master needs disciples because they are like his hands, his limbs, the expansion of his own consciousness. And when he gets the command from the Highest, then he has to try to find those who are going to be part and parcel of his consciousness to help him fulfil the command.

Traditionally, spiritual Masters used to say, "If you have something, others are bound to come. The pond does not go to the thirsty person; the thirsty person comes to the pond." This is absolutely true if a mature person is thirsty. But if you feel that the thirsty person is just an infant, then it is all different. The baby will cry in his room, and the mother will have to come running to feed him. The mother does not say to the baby, "You have to come to me, since you want something from me." No, the mother puts everything aside and comes to the baby. In the spiritual world also, some Masters feel the need to go out into the world, for the outer world is just a baby in consciousness. These Masters feel that there are many children who are crying for spiritual life, spiritual wisdom, spiritual perfection, but who do not know where or how to find it. So the Masters go from place to place and offer their Light with the idea of serving the divinity in humanity. I happen to be one of those. I move around because I feel that there are sincere children who need the Light that the Supreme has given me to offer to mankind. That is why I go to Japan, to Europe, and all over the United States— because I feel that the outer world is my child.

When the world is crying, if we have the capacity, we have to feed it. If I have the capacity to give you something and I also have the capacity to go and stand right in front of you, why do I have to call you to me? If I have the capacity both to place myself before you and to give you the light that you want, then I must do so. If I do not have the capacity, then I have to keep silent.

If a person who calls himself a realised

soul feels the necessity and has the capacity, then let him go out into the world to prove God's existence. If he has the capacity but does not feel the necessity, then let him stay where he is. If he neither feels the necessity nor has the capacity to show God to the world, then let him not try to prove his aspiration and demonstrate his emotion. Why? Because God does not want him to do this. He is not fulfilling God in God's way, but making a parade of himself before humanity and broadcasting himself before God. Before the world's eye, he is undesirable; before God's Eye, he is unpardonable.

The outer world is very limited in comparison to the inner world. The length and breadth of the outer world is no more than a few thousand miles, but the inner world is without limit. A spiritual person feels, on the strength of his own realisation, that all worlds are his, because his Master, the Supreme, is all-pervading. Now, if the Supreme is all-pervading, then why is it beneath the dignity of His son to go from one place to another?

There are various ways to feed the world. Writing is one way; giving talks is another. If one has many capacities, why should he not use all of them? Some spiritual Masters do not have these outer capacities. Sri Ramakrishna, for example, did not write. But that did not prevent him from realising the Highest. At the same time, those who have the capacity to write and give talks are not deprived of their God-realisation.

God plays in various ways. If God gives a spiritual Master the capacity to write, to give talks, to mix with people, to travel from place to place, then that is God's business. It is God's Will that the Master is carrying out. And if God does not give the Master the capacity to write and speak, we cannot blame that spiritual Master or say he is inferior. We have to know what God wants from us. If God wants me to write, He will give me the capacity. If God does not want you to write, He will not give you the capacity. In neither case can we find fault. But unfortunately, our traditional India has been very, very narrow-minded in this matter.

Question: Once you said that when a seeker reaches the highest realisation, automatically spiritual manifestation comes. Would you explain to me what you mean by that kind of manifestation?

Sri Chinmoy: When one gets realisation, if he remains in the world, automatically manifestation starts. When you stand in front of a liberated, fully realised soul, what happens? Immediately you see the vast difference between yourself and that person. The first thing you see in him is Peace; in his eyes you will see infinite Peace. From his body you will get a sense of Purity, a Purity which you have never felt before in your life or in anybody else's life. How is it that he is emanating Purity, Light and divine Power, while somebody else is not? It is just because he is fully realised. He is not talking to you, he is not saying anything to you, but from his very presence you get infinite Peace, infinite Bliss, infinite Light. So realisation automatically shows its own capacity, which is manifestation. The inner realisation of the Master is being manifested through his outer form, which is the body.

There is another kind of manifestation, which we find more on the physical plane: it is the manifestation of divinity on earth. This manifestation takes place when a spiritual Master deliberately tries to awaken spiritually hungry individuals. There are many people on earth who are spiritually hungry, but they do not have a Master or a spiritual path. So the Master tries to inspire them and kindle the flame of conscious aspiration in them and put them on a spiritual path.

When a spiritual Master, with the help of his dearest disciples, tries to manifest divinity on earth, sometimes people misunderstand him. They think he wants to convert everyone. But the Master's motive is not that of a missionary. Christian missionaries went to India and all over the world, saying, "There is only one saviour, the Christ." But if the Christ is the only saviour, then where does the Buddha stand? Where does Sri Krishna stand? Where are Sri Ramakrishna and all the other great Masters? Each genuine spiritual Master is a saviour, needless to say; but to say that he is the *only* saviour, or that his path is the *only* path, is foolishness. If I say that my path is the only path, that if you do not accept me you will go to hell, then there is no more stupid person on earth than I. In our path, we do not convert anybody; we inspire. Many of you here are not my disciples and are not going to be my disciples. But I am most glad that you have come and most grateful to you for your presence here. I have the capacity, through God's Grace, to inspire you. You may take my inspiration and then go to whatever path you need or want. I have played my part by inspiring you.

A realised Master never, never tries to convert; he only offers his realisation in the form of inspiration to aspiring souls. That is why the Master has to act like a normal human being. If he does not act like a human being, if he does not eat and take rest and talk in a human way, then people will say, "Oh, you have gone far beyond us. It is simply impossible for us to be like you." But the spiritual Master says, "No, I do everything you do. If I can eat the same food, if I can mix with you the way you mix with others and, at the same time, not lose my highest consciousness, then how is it that you also cannot enter into the Highest?" This is how the Master inspires his disciples.

But inspiration is not enough. After inspiration comes aspiration. There is a great difference, a vast difference, between inspiration and aspiration. Aspiration is very, very high. The spiritual Master becomes one with his disciples, whose aspiration he has already helped, and together they go to inspire the spiritually hungry world. In this way realisation is transformed into manifestation.

When there is realisation, inside the realisation you will see manifestation. Manifestation is the outer form of realisation, and one who is really spiritual will immediately feel the manifestation in the realisation itself. For ordinary people, for humanity, it takes time. If I have realised something and manifested it in the outer world, the heart of humanity feels it, but the physical mind may take a little time to perceive and understand the manifestation. In the field of manifestation, the Master is dealing with ignorant, unaspiring people or emotionally bound people who will not see the Master's full Light. But a great aspirant sees the realisation and cannot separate the realisation from the manifestation.

Question: What is the difference between revelation and manifestation?

Sri Chinmoy: First we have embodiment. Inside your pocket—which means inside you—is a most delicious mango. You put your hand inside the pocket and bring out the mango and show it to me. This is revelation. Before, the mango was concealed, and now you have revealed it. Then you have to manifest it. How will you do that? You will cut it into a few pieces and share it with me and with others.

When you reveal God or Truth or Light to the world, it means that you have brought these things forward and they are there for all the world to see. But if nobody looks at what you have revealed, or if nobody accepts or understands it, then this is revelation without manifestation. Manifestation means not only to show what you have and what you are, but also to make the world see, feel, understand and accept it. This is the difference. Today's realisation is tomorrow's revelation. Revelation is today's manifested realisation and tomorrow's fulfilled manifestation.

Question: Can a spiritual Master who tries to reveal the higher truths be compared in some ways to a poet who tries to express and reveal artistic truths?

Sri Chinmoy: An ordinary poet may get a glimpse of the truth, but the spiritual Masters get the ocean of Truth itself. Spiritual Masters see a much higher truth than any ordinary poets see. Also, in the case of ordinary poets, poetry is everything to them. But in the case of advanced souls or spiritual Masters, poetry is not everything; God is everything.

The poet who brings down higher messages feels that these are everything he has to give. But spiritual Masters feel that their writings represent absolutely nothing when compared with what they know and what they truly are. They say, "In comparison to my realisation, my manifestation is absolutely nothing. The Light that I have offered, when compared with the Light that is still unmanifested, is nothing. If, for my realisation, I get one hundred out of one hundred, for my manifestation I will not get more than one out of one hundred. When I die, I know how much inner wealth will never have a chance to manifest through me." All spiritual Masters have been frustrated this way in their expression, in their revelation, in their manifestation.

Question: Why is it that realised Gurus sometimes seem to defy the scriptures and accepted rules in what they say and do?

Sri Chinmoy: It is true that realised Gurus, great Gurus, have their own truth. But they do not defy anything. What they do is give a new orientation. Suppose a great spiritual figure has said something. At the time that he lived, that particular truth was needed. But the world is progressing, and now some higher truth must be manifested. So if we say something different, we are not defying the great Masters of the past. What we are doing is bringing a higher truth and a higher knowledge into the earth-consciousness, which is now ready to receive it. We are enlarging and illumining the truth.

Only by entering into the truth and transforming it will we achieve a larger and wider truth. If we think that everything to be said with regard to spirituality has already been spoken by our forefathers, we are mistaken. Truth is never complete because we are living in an ever-transcending universe. What the teachers of the past have said is eternally true; what we are saying is also eternally true. But each truth has its own grade, and all the time we are evolving and progressing.

Your father might have imagined or thought of something on the physical plane which was at the time quite striking. Now you have grown up, and you are thinking of something higher and deeper because science has evolved to a new plane. That does not mean that you are defying the achievements of your father. No, you are going beyond him, beyond his capacity, beyond his understanding.

In the spiritual life we do not negate; we just go higher and higher to reach the topmost height. Still the highest Truth, the topmost realisation, or what we call the absolute manifestation, has not taken place. Spiritual manifestation has not been completed, and perhaps it will never be completed.

Question: There were a number of spiritual Masters who used to smoke and drink. How did they realise God?

Sri Chinmoy: It was because of their aspiration. Spiritual Masters used to drink, dance, eat meat and do all kinds of things without losing their height. For them the world was like a garden, and they were divine children playing there unaffected by anything they said or did.

But you have to know that there is a little difference between their aspiration and yours. It is like the difference between you and a tree. A tree does no harm to anyone; it is pure and innocent. But you will realise God long before the tree does. When it is a matter of inner cry, of aspiration, an ordinary person cannot compare himself with the great spiritual Masters. Once they started meditating, they could go on for hours and become lost in their meditation.

Many Indian spiritual Masters take arsenic, and sometimes when they take large quantities people think they are going to commit suicide. But it does not harm them. Some of the *tantric* Yogis lead such a life of vital pleasure that anyone would think they would fall immediately. But their meditation surpasses their vital life. When they are on the verge of realisation, all the time their consciousness is in a very high world and they do not remain in the physical at all, so they realise God in spite of their vital life. Similarly, some occultists meditate for nine or ten hours daily, and the rest of the time they lead a very bad life. But the intensity of their aspiration brings them realisation anyway.

Question: Do spiritual Masters usually take birth in very spiritual families?

Sri Chinmoy: Most of the real spiritual Masters entered into very highly developed, spiritual families. In their case, it was God's plan. But God is not bound by any plan; God may send a spiritual Master into a most unaspiring family. That is also possible. But in most cases, spiritual Masters do come into spiritual families.

Question: What is the difference between a Yogi and an Avatar?

Sri Chinmoy: A Yogi is a fully realised soul. Higher than a realised soul is a partial or incomplete Avatar, an *Angsha* Avatar. Higher than a partial Avatar is a full Avatar, a *Purna* Avatar. A Yogi can deal with a few people, a section of humanity; an Avatar can deal with the entire world. A Yogi silently acts; an Avatar acts dynamically and speaks confidently. A Yogi is a plant; an Avatar is a huge, tall tree.

An Avatar is a direct descendant of God: a real, solid portion of the Divine which constantly operates in the Highest and also in the lowest. An Avatar has the capacity of a huge sea, while a Yogi has the capacity of a river or a pool. When Yogis want to raise the consciousness of humanity, they will sometimes be affected by the ignorance of the earth. But an Avatar will remain in the Highest and the lowest together, and even in his lowest, his ability to function is not affected. An Avatar has infinitely more capacity than a Yogi in bringing about the total transformation of humanity.

Again, even an Avatar of the highest order may not or cannot function always from the highest level of consciousness because of the world's ignorance, darkness and imperfection. The earth's consciousness is not aspiring, and most human beings do not want his Light. Look at the Christ. Who cared for him? Very few! Look at Sri Krishna. Who accepted him? Very few!

According to Indian philosophy and spiritual teachings, an Avatar is a direct descendant of the Supreme who can commune with Him directly at will. Most of the Yogis cannot do that; it will take them two or three hours to enter into their highest consciousness in order to commune with God. Communion with God in the twinkling of an eye they do not have. Only the Avatar's communion with God is of this type.

An Avatar is a human being; he talks, eats, breathes and does everything else like a human being. But when he enters into his highest, if ever you can have even a glimpse of his consciousness, your whole life will be an object of complete surrender at his feet. Even if he kicks you, throws you aside, you will remain like a faithful dog, because in him you have got a matchless treasure which nobody else on earth will be able to give you. One has to have a very, very high standard of spiritual consciousness in order to get even the faintest glimpse of an Avatar's height. His consciousness can never be expressed or explained.

To have an Avatar as one's Guru is to have the greatest blessing that man can ever have. Sri Ramakrishna used to say, "If God is a cow, then the udder, which gives the milk, is the Avatar." A great aspirant will say that God in the form of an Avatar is more compassionate than God Himself. The aspirant says, "If I do something wrong, in God's case there is judgement, there is the law of Karma. But with the Guru, it is different. He has only deep affection for his dearest disciples. So when the actual punishment comes to me, the Guru will take the punishment." If the seeker prays to God and cries to God most sincerely and powerfully, then God may forgive him instead of punishing him. But if one has an Avatar as his Guru, and if he has the closest connection with the Avatar, then this Guru actually takes the punishment on the disciple's behalf.

Also, when there is one Avatar on earth, he embodies the consciousness of all other Avatars that came before him. Sri Ramakrishna said, "He who is Rama, he who is Krishna, in one form is Ramakrishna." In the West, unfortunately, you recognise only the Christ as an Avatar. Either you accept him or you reject him. If you accept him, then there can be no other for you. But in this you are making a mistake. The Christ, the Buddha, Sri Krishna and others all came from the same room. If you take the Christ as the divine, infinite Consciousness, then you cannot separate Sri Krishna, the Buddha or Sri Ramakrishna from the Christ. The Supreme entered into the form which you call the Christ; He entered into the form which you call Sri Krishna; He entered into the form which you call Sri Ramakrishna.

Question: Was Vivekananda an Avatar?

Sri Chinmoy: Vivekananda was not an Avatar. He had only a few glimpses of the Truth that Sri Ramakrishna lived. Sri Ramakrishna lived the highest Truth, and Vivekananda had glimpses of that Truth. Vivekananda was a great *Vibhuti,* one who is endowed with a special power of God, who acts most dynamically in the world-atmosphere. *Vibhutis* are leaders of mankind who awaken the slumbering consciousness.

We cannot call Napoleon a *Vibhuti,* but what Napoleon accomplished in the material world, Vivekananda accomplished in the spiritual world. The most powerful, dynamic power acted in human form in Vivekananda. Vivekananda's real mission was to spread the message of his Master, Sri Ramakrishna. Ramakrishna achieved, but he did not manifest much. He did not care for worldly achievement or the so-called manifold development. The present-day world needs the mind. The mind need not even be intellectual; it may be just an ordinary mind that can understand basic things. But Sri Ramakrishna did not care even for this ordinary mind. So Vivekananda collected the fruits of the tree that was Ramakrishna and offered them to the world. He came to the West at the age of thirty and brought abundant light to the West.

At the time of Sri Ramakrishna's passing, Vivekananda still doubted his Master's spiritual height. He said inwardly, "If you tell me that you are a great Avatar, I will believe." So Ramakrishna read his mind and said, "Naren, you still doubt me? He who is Rama, he who is Krishna, in one form in this body is Ramakrishna." Rama was an Avatar, Krishna was an Avatar, and Vivekananda's Master embodied them both.

Vivekananda was not an Avatar; he cannot be put on the same footing with Sri Ramakrishna. I have great love and admiration for Vivekananda. My connection with him in the inner world is very close. Unfortunately, here in the West I encounter some spiritual people and swamis who belittle Vivekananda and his achievement, and dare to say he was not realised. But all I can say is that those who belittle Vivekananda are not worthy of washing his feet. God-realisation he certainly had; he was very advanced.

The height of an Avatar cannot be judged by an ordinary person. It is like a dwarf trying to scale the height of a giant; it is ridiculous. But let us not think of a spiritual Master's height. Let us only think of his presence in our heart. When we can feel his presence in the depth of our heart, he can be our help, our guide, our inspiration, our aspiration, our journey and our Goal.

Question: How do you personally know whether someone is realised or partially realised?

Sri Chinmoy: When one is realised, one can easily know the realisation of others. On the basis of my unity and identification with their consciousness, I can easily tell about others' realisation.

Question: Am I correct in saying that the Buddha is one of those who advocated a kind of escape from the world?

Sri Chinmoy: If you say that the Buddha's philosophy is one of escape, that he consciously wanted to have an escape, that would be wrong; it is a misinterpretation. What the Buddha actually wanted was to put an end to human suffering in the world. Like a divine warrior, he played his part on the world-scene. He did not use the term 'God', but he used the terms 'Truth' and 'Light'. He stayed on earth for forty years after his own realisation, trying to elevate the consciousness of humanity. He went here and there, always preaching, preaching. Even though he had such a frail body, he went on giving talks and trying to bring down peace, light and bliss. But he saw that the people he was trying to help were not receiving, and he came to feel that it was almost impossible to end human suffering.

Then he discovered there is something called *nirvana,* where all desires are extinguished, where all earthly propensities are extinguished, where all limitations are extinguished. There you go beyond the domain of the physical, and all is inner existence. So he said, "Now I am very, very tired. Let me enter into that blissful state and take rest." He decided to let other divine soldiers come into the world to fight for the full manifestation. Now, if one soldier fights bravely for many years and then takes rest, and if another soldier coming after him decides to keep on fighting until he can manifest the Highest, naturally we feel that this second person is playing his role with more strength, more energy, more sta-

mina. If one wants to manifest after realisation, naturally he is leading humanity
one step ahead, because manifestation
God also needs.

But to say that the one person did not play
his role or wanted to escape is wrong. As an
individual, the Buddha did play his role.
Realisation the Buddha had. Revelation he
had. He also started manifesting, but
ultimately he did not want to play a conscious
part in the field of manifestation. He did not
want to participate in the cosmic Play any
more. Some of the Buddha's followers
misunderstood his philosophy and twisted it to
their own sweet satisfaction. As an individual,
the Buddha never advocated escape or
negating the world. What he advocated was
prayer and meditation to enter into the
everlasting blissful state of consciousness. You
can say he opened up another path, or you can
call it a house. Those who enter into that
particular path or house do not come back
into the world after God-realisation, whereas
those who enter into some other house *do*
come back to the world.

It is not that if you enter into *nirvana* you are
caught there. No, if you enter into *nirvana*,
usually you do not come back because you do
not want to. But there are some Masters who

go beyond the state of *nirvana* and do return to the world. They do not stay in the house. The dynamic urge of the Supreme compels these Masters to come back into the world again even after they have lived one life as a God-realised soul, to work for His manifestation.

Question: What is nirvana?

Sri Chinmoy:

"No mind, no form, I only exist;
Now ceased all will and thought.
The final end of Nature's dance,
I am It whom I have sought.

. . . .

I barter nothing with time and deeds;
My cosmic play is done."

— from *The Absolute*
by Sri Chinmoy

When one's cosmic play is done, he enters into *nirvana*. If one is a tired soul and wants to go permanently beyond the conflict, beyond the capacities of the cosmic forces, then *nirvana* is to be welcomed. *Nirvana* is the cessation of all earthly activities, the extinction of desires, suffering, bondage, limitation and death. In this state one goes beyond the conception of time and space. This world, earth, is the playground for the dance of the cosmic forces. But when one enters into *nirvana,* the cosmic forces yield to the ultimate highest Truth, and the Knower, the Known and the Knowledge or Wisdom are like three angels blended into one. At that time one becomes both the Knower and the Known.

If one does not have the experience of *nirvana,* he usually cannot know what illusion is. According to some spiritual teachers, the world is *maya,* an illusion. When one enters into *nirvana,* he realises what illusion is. *Nirvana* is the static oneness with God. There, everything comes to an end in the static Bliss. This Bliss is unimaginable, unfathomable, indescribable. Beyond *nirvana* is the state of absolute oneness. This oneness is the dynamic oneness with God.

Nirvana is a very, very, very high state. However, it is not the highest state for the divine worker. If one wants to serve God here on earth, then he has to come back into the world again and again to serve the Supreme in humanity. If one wants to manifest the Supreme in the field of creation, then he has to work in the absolute dynamism of the Supreme, and not take rest in *nirvana.* This does not mean that the divine worker cannot have the experience of *nirvana*. The experience of *nirvana* is at the command of all God-realised souls. But permanent *nirvana* is for those who want to be satisfied with the static aspect of the supreme Brahman. If one wants to embody both the static and dynamic aspects of the Supreme, then I wish to say that one should go beyond *nirvana* and enter into the field of manifestation.

Question: Is there any difference between nirvana *and* nirvikalpa *samadhi?*

Sri Chinmoy: Let us take *nirvana* and *nirvikalpa* samadhi as two tallest mansions. Other mansions are next to nothing in comparison to these two mansions. If you climb up the *nirvana*-mansion, there is no way to come down, or you do not feel the necessity of coming down to offer what you have recieved to the world. There is no link with the earth-consciousness. In *nirvana* you notice the extinction of earth-pangs and the end of the cosmic dance. *Nirvana* is flooded with infinite Peace and Bliss. From the point of view of Absolute Truth, *nirvana* is the Goal of goals to the seekers who do not want to take any more part in God's manifested creation. Of course, if the Supreme Pilot wants an individual seeker of the absolute Truth to go beyond *nirvana* and enter into the world for earth-transformation and earth-perfection in a divine way, He sends him down. He feels that that particular instrument of His is supremely indispensable for transforming the Supreme's birthless transcendental Vision into His deathless universal Reality.

When you climb up the *nirvikalpa* samadhi-mansion, there is a way to climb down if you want to. But if you stay there for a long period of time, then you totally forget that there is a way to come down. *Nirvikalpa* samadhi throws illumination-flood into us and makes us feel that there are higher worlds far beyond this world of ours. Further, it reveals itself to the seeker as a connecting link between this world and other high, higher, highest worlds, and it offers him the road to go beyond it and enter into the ever-transcending Beyond.

ABOUT SRI CHINMOY

Sri Chinmoy was born in Bengal, India in 1931. At the age of twelve he entered an ashram, or religious community, where he spent the next twenty years practising meditation and intense spiritual disciplines. During this period, he underwent a series of profound religious experiences and achieved a state of enlightenment called God-realisation.

In 1964 he came to America to offer the fruits of his realisations to the aspiring Western consciousness. Since then he has established spiritual centres throughout the United States, Canada, Western Europe and Australia. He has published several books on meditation and spirituality and has been invited to lecture at the world's great universities — including Oxford, Cambridge, Harvard, Yale and Tokyo. He conducts meditations twice a week for United Nations delegates and staff at the

Church Center for the United Nations and the U.N. Headquarters in New York, and delivers the monthly Dag Hammarskjold Lecture Series there. Daily meditations by Sri Chinmoy are broadcast by radio stations around the country, and a number of television stations air his early morning services on a regular basis.

For information on other books by Sri Chinmoy, please contact:

Sri Chinmoy
P. O. Box 32433
Jamaica, N.Y. 11431

For additional books by Sri Chinmoy
please write to:

Sri Chinmoy
P. O. Box 32433
Jamaica, N.Y. 11431

Astrology, the Supernatural and the Beyond. A well-known Yogi and spiritual Master answers questions on astrology, the occult, psychic power, the supernatural and other cosmic forces influencing man.

paperback, $2.00

Beyond Within. A 500-page anthology of essays, discourses, stories, poems and aphorisms collected from Sri Chinmoy's writings during his ten years in the West. In this book, an illumined Yogi discusses topics such as the human psyche, meditation, will, consciousness and the higher worlds of Bliss and Light.

paperback, $6.95

Colour Kingdom. A spiritual Master of the highest order uses his own occult vision to reveal the occult meaning and significance of the different colours and shades of colour. It can be used as a practical guide for meditation and concentration exercises. Includes 51 coloured illustrations.

paperback, $5.00

Death and Reincarnation: Eternity's Voyage. A spiritual Master who has journeyed during meditation to the different planes of reality answers questions on death, reincarnation and life after death.

paperback, $2.00

Kundalini: The Mother-Power. A series of lectures on Kundalini Yoga and the awakening of hidden occult forces within man through meditation, concentration and other spiritual practices.

paperback, $2.00

Sri Chinmoy Primer. A general introduction to the spiritual life, dealing with the kinds of questions that new disciples and seekers most frequently ask a spiritual Master. Here Sri Chinmoy answers questions on meditation, mantras, diet, breathing, sex, how to choose a Guru and spiritual initiation.

paperback, $1.00

Yoga and the Spiritual Life. A comprehensive practical explanation of Yoga philosophy. Covers all aspects of the spiritual life with questions and answers on meditation and the soul.

paperback, $2.50